a Parent's Guide to
Raising Money-Sm
kids

AUTHOR
Robin Taub, CA

ILLUSTRATOR
Farida Zaman

CA
Chartered Accountants
of Canada

Financial
Decisions
Matter

Library and Archives Canada Cataloguing in Publication

Taub, Robin
    A parent's guide to raising money smart kids / Robin Taub.

(Financial literacy)
ISBN 978-1-55385-596-5

    1. Children--Finance, Personal. 2. Teenagers--Finance, Personal.   I. Canadian Institute of Chartered Accountants   II. Title.   III. Series: Financial literacy (Toronto, Ont.)

HG179.T375 2011   332.0240083   C2011-905160-5

Copyright © 2011
The Canadian Institute of Chartered Accountants
277 Wellington Street West
Toronto ON M5V 3H2

Printed and bound in Canada

FOREWORD

The Canadian Institute of Chartered Accountants recently commissioned research about the level of financial literacy in Canada, and the results—consistent with the research and recommendations of the Federal Task Force on Financial Literacy—were a wake-up call: Canadians need to improve their financial literacy skills!

If you are like most Canadians, you believe that responsible money management is an important life skill—and one that should be taught to kids. The research shows that most parents feel it's their responsibility to teach their kids about money management, and many have tried. But a vast majority of parents feel they have not been very successful at it. They feel they don't have the information they need, and they don't know how to approach the subject with kids of different ages. They recognize that they need help and they are willing to listen and learn. That's why this book was written. We believe that the earlier kids are taught, the greater the likelihood of their financial success throughout life.

As chartered accountants, we know about money. We hope this book will give you the information and skills you need to communicate effectively with your children about important money matters. We hope that it will also make you more aware of your own behaviour around money and the type of financial role model you are to your kids currently—and the type of role model you can become. It may also lead to improvements in your own financial health as you become more skilled in understanding, practising, and explaining money management. Finally, we hope it will help your kids feel more confident about their financial decisions.

Kevin Dancey, FCA
President & CEO
The Canadian Institute of Chartered Accountants

TABLE OF CONTENTS

CHAPTER 2: TEACHING YOUNG CHILDREN

CHAPTER 3: TEACHING PRE-TEENS

CHAPTER 4: TEACHING TEENAGERS

CHAPTER 5: TEACHING EMERGING ADULTS

INTRODUCTION

To get the most out of your reading, you should understand a few things about how the book is organized. The first chapter sets the stage, explaining why it's important to help your kids become money-smart. It also covers what that implies about your own responsibility to be smart with your money so that you can teach by example, because a good example really is the best teacher.

But beyond your own example there is the very basic need to talk to your kids about money. How do you approach it? We've given a lot of thought to this question, and the conclusion we've reached is that there are really five basic aspects of money that can be used to structure an ongoing conversation. First there's the fact that in order to have money you have to earn it. Then, once you've earned it, there are really just four things to do with it:

* Save
* Spend
* Share
* Invest.

Chapters 2 through 5 are directed to parents with kids at different stages—young children (5 to 8 years old), pre-teens (9 to 12 years old), teens (13 to 17 years old), and emerging adults (18 to 21 years old). Each chapter is organized around the five aspects of money just discussed—**Earn**, **Save**, **Spend**, **Share** and **Invest**. There are suggestions for family discussions and activities designed to reinforce these concepts. Each chapter also contains quotes from parents talking about how they approached financial literacy with their kids, quotes that sometimes remind us that there is often humour even in the most serious topics.

We hope that the suggestions in this book, and the real-life experiences of other parents, will make your conversations with your kids easier and more effective. We also welcome your ideas and anecdotes. Please email us at: **moneysmartkids@cica.ca**

1

"Dad, how much money do you make?"

Getting to Money Smart

UNDERSTANDING HOW KIDS LEARN ABOUT MONEY

This first chapter is about understanding the context in which kids learn about money; it discusses some of the problem areas that parents run into and suggests approaches to deal with the problems effectively. It also discusses a number of "Healthy Habits of Financial Management" that can help you achieve two objectives: getting your own finances in order and teaching your kids how to do the same.

WHY IS IT IMPORTANT TO RAISE MONEY-SMART KIDS?

We all want to raise our kids to be healthy, happy, successful adults. We want them to be able to manage their lives well, including their financial lives, for their sake as well as our own. If we don't succeed in teaching our kids about money management, it may come back to haunt us. How would you feel, for instance, if you had to support your *adult* children financially? Or if you had to bail them out of a financial mess with savings painstakingly accumulated and set aside for your own future? What if this happened when you were supposed to be enjoying your care-free retirement years? It's not a pretty picture, is it?

Those are some of the potential consequences for us as parents, but what about the kids themselves? Healthy, happy and successful adults, among other things, are adults who are financially responsible and independent. If you've ever struggled with financial problems that were brought on by bad habits—or simply by not knowing how to approach financial management effectively and efficiently—then you know what a negative impact such problems can have on your life generally, and especially on your relationships with the people closest to you. Certainly it's worth our effort to save our children from such a fate.

A neighbour has a 26-year-old daughter who lives at home with her parents. She only has a part-time job working in retail, spends $4 every four hours on fancy coffees, buys take-out food regularly for dinner and just came home from a week's vacation in Mexico. And she doesn't have

any savings at all—no RRSP, no TFSA, not even a basic savings account. The worst part is she could care less about learning about finances—she is more concerned about how many friends she has on Facebook!

Her parents now bemoan the fact that they did not take the time to teach their daughter good money management skills and habits when she was younger. They are distressed by the fact that she does not seem to share any of their values and seems to take so much for granted. It's really strained their relationship with her.

WHAT ARE THE CHALLENGES TO RAISING MONEY-SMART KIDS?

The basic challenges parents face are lack of knowledge, lack of time and lack of opportunity (or not always recognizing when an opportunity presents itself). Teaching your kids how to manage money is particularly hard if you're not good at it yourself. It becomes really easy to just avoid the conversations altogether, especially when you're running a busy household with so many competing demands on your time. Although it may not feel like a priority when your kids are little, their early years are an important time to lay the foundation and teach the basics. The concepts are the same as they get older, but the stakes get much higher. It's better if they can learn from their mistakes when the stakes are low.

A lot of parents procrastinate: they don't teach their kids about money because they think their kids are too young. But there are lots of ways to engage younger children with money. Maybe your kids don't seem all that interested in learning about money. Your challenge is to make it relevant to them, and use opportunities in your everyday lives as teachable moments. You don't have to set aside extra time; these opportunities will crop up in day-to-day activities like grocery shopping, planning a birthday party and going to the mall, as well as when they get their first "real" job.

What if your kids are already teenagers but you've never taught them about money; is it too late? No — it's never too late to learn a new skill or to learn how to do things better. The way you approach money management with teens is different. For instance, you can discuss more sophisticated topics with them than with their younger siblings. But the basic concepts are the same throughout your kids' lives and your own: when you **EARN** money, you have four basic choices about what to do with it: **SAVE**, **SPEND**, **SHARE** and **INVEST**. You want your kids to understand that making a lot of money does not guarantee financial security; financial security comes from making sound decisions with the money you make.

WHAT KIND OF FINANCIAL ROLE MODEL ARE YOU?

As parents, you try to be good role models for your children. You are careful about how you treat and relate to others, how you look after your health and well-being, and how you balance work and family life, because you know your kids observe everything. They are watching and learning from you — and they pick up both your good and bad habits, including habits of financial management. So, what kind of financial role model are you? Do you spend money impulsively or are you cautious and deliberate about your spending? Do you save up for a big purchase or do you buy what you want when you want it, charge it to your credit card and worry about it later? Do you pay your bills on time and keep organized files or do you throw unopened bills on top of the fridge and ignore them? Try doing the Role Model Self-Assessment exercise at the end of this chapter; it will give you a good idea of where you stand as a role model. And if you teach your kids well, you'll find that older siblings can also be important role models for younger kids.

IS MONEY A TABOO TOPIC IN YOUR HOME?

In many households, money is a taboo topic. Some parents would rather talk to their kids about sex than about money! Many parents say they avoid talking about money with their kids because they don't feel qualified to do it properly. They don't know how to approach it and they don't have the information they need. Many also feel they are not equipped to handle some of the uncomfortable questions that their kids may ask, like: "Are we rich?" "How much money do you make?" and "How much is our mortgage?" The answers to these questions are private family

"Dad, how much money do you make?"

matters and probably not something you want to share with the whole world, so you have to keep in mind your child's age and maturity when answering them. Ask your kid questions to make sure you understand what they are really asking. Often when kids ask such questions, they're really just looking for reassurance that everything's okay. But if they ask, it's best to find an answer that is honest, one that stresses confidentiality and trust, and one that is only as detailed as you think appropriate. The discussion can often take place by dealing with general concepts rather than getting into specific numbers — concepts such as the meaning of "rich"; the importance of income, i.e., not that it be a certain amount but that it is sufficient to provide a stable life; how mortgages work and good debt vs. bad debt.

While it may be taboo to expose confidential family information, there should be nothing distasteful about teaching your kids general money management skills. Talking about living within your means, budgeting or saving for important goals should be discussed openly. And it should be discussed often.

THE BIG PICTURE: HOUSEHOLD FINANCES

One of the goals of teaching your kids about money is to make them aware of the cost of running a household. Not that your kids should feel responsible for making ends meet — that's your job as a head of the household. But they can at least become aware of the cost of their needs and wants and get a better understanding of how providing for them fits into the bigger picture. Kids, especially teenagers, can seem selfish because they tend to focus only on their own needs (and wants). With more information, though, they will come to realize that you have to prioritize and balance all of the family's costs of living. It helps them put things in the proper perspective.

Budgeting: Overhead expenses and discretionary spending

Raising kids is expensive. According to MSN Money's Gordon Powers, the estimated cost of raising a child in Canada from birth to adulthood ranges from

$193,000 to $250,000. And these costs are just some of the components of your household budget. For some families, budgeting is a dreaded activity, right up there with dieting! Both words bring up thoughts of deprivation. But if you think of a budget as a spending plan, one that will let you have and do the things in life that are most important to you and that are aligned with your values, it makes an otherwise tedious process meaningful and rewarding.

When creating a spending plan, keep in mind that your expenses fall into two broad categories, overhead expenses and discretionary spending. Most overhead expenses are fixed costs and are governed by a contract. They are easier to plan for than variable expenses because they usually cost the same amount every month (though some fixed costs, such as annual home insurance premiums, are periodic or occasional). These expenses cannot really be avoided because they are the basic costs of living. Examples are rent or mortgage payments, property taxes, car payments or other transportation costs, and cable bills. Other overhead expenses like groceries, clothing, utilities and gas for the car are a bit more variable — the amount you spend may change from month to month, but you cannot eliminate these expenses altogether.

Discretionary expenses, as the name suggests, are costs incurred at your discretion. You have a lot of flexibility as to whether to incur these costs at all, and if you do, how much to spend. Examples include restaurant meals and entertainment, "recreational shopping", personal care, vacations, club dues, hobbies and gifts.

So, how to budget? The initial step is to *pay yourself first* by automatically transferring a certain sum of money every month to a designated account. Depending on your goals and objectives, this can be either a regular savings account or a tax-sheltered account like a Registered Retirement Savings Plan (RRSP) or a Tax-Free Savings Account (TFSA). You get used to living without this money, and what remains after you've paid yourself first goes towards covering your overhead expenses. Any funds that remain after you cover all of your overhead are available for discretionary spending or additional savings.

Use the Cash Flow Calculator at the end of this chapter to calculate your household cash flow. Most likely the biggest cash outflow in your budget is your mortgage payment, followed by car payments, property tax, insurance and possibly tuition. You can use the Cash Flow Calculator to create a spending plan that's right for you and your family.

Closing a financial gap

Preparing your budget and your cash flow will give you a clear picture of your financial health. If you are spending less than you earn, your cash flow will be positive. That positive cash flow is money for savings (or sometimes for further discretionary spending). If, on the other hand, you are spending more than you make, your cash flow will be negative. Most people deal with negative cash flow by using credit to cover the shortfall. For example, they may use credit cards, department store cards, personal lines of credit or home equity lines of credit. Using credit occasionally because your household cash flow is uneven, (e.g., you are self-employed or earn commissions) is fine. In those situations, you may run surpluses (excess cash flow) some months and deficits (insufficient cash flow) other months. But if you are using credit every month to make ends meet, then you are living beyond your means. You are also building up debt as those monthly shortfalls begin to accumulate. This situation is obviously not sustainable. In his book, *Client-Centred Life Planning*,[1] Michael R. Curtis introduces the following "Three C" strategies to close a financial gap:

- **Create**: creating additional income or wealth
- **Convert**: converting consumption assets into income-producing assets
- **Conserve**: conserving existing resources.

You can use these strategies alone or together. Always look for high-leverage solutions that will have a significant impact on the bottom line. For instance, if you can't afford your monthly car payments, conserving by cutting back on your daily latte may help a bit, but it probably won't get you all the way there!

---

1   Toronto, Canada: Michael R. Curtis, 2005

Create	Creating wealth brings more cash into the household. For some people, this may mean returning to the paid labour force or turning a passion or hobby into a business. For others, it may mean adjusting their investment portfolio to focus more on generating income to supplement their salary.
Convert	Downsizing to a smaller house is the classic example of the "Convert" strategy and has been a popular strategy as people move into their retirement years. Selling your large family home, buying a less expensive, smaller home and investing the difference allows you to convert a consumption asset into an income-producing asset. Converting may also involve the sale of a cottage or other vacation property, boats, cars or other unnecessary assets to generate capital that can be invested to produce income or meet other financial objectives.
Conserve	Creating and converting are long- and medium-term solutions, but conserving has immediate impact. Examine your expenses for ways to defer, cut back or eliminate excessive or unnecessary spending. Look for the discretionary expenses like meals, entertainment, shopping and vacations that are easy to cut.

If you take these tips to heart, you can rest assured that you will become exactly the kind of role model your kids need to make them money-smart—both now and throughout their lives.

HOW YOUR VALUES INFLUENCE YOUR FINANCIAL DECISIONS

Values are the things in your life that are most important to you, that you are willing to take a stand for. Some people value education, achievement, prestige or wealth. Others value security, family, friendship or adventure. The way you spend your money and deal with your finances says a lot about your values. Do you know what your top five values are? Do the Values Validator exercise at the end of this chapter and find out.

You may think your kids will pick up your values about money by osmosis, but these days kids are exposed to a lot of conflicting messages about money, especially from the media and their friends. So be clear and explicit about your family values and how they impact your financial decisions. Get your kids to try the Values Validator, and leave their answers out in the kitchen where everyone can see them. Let the list be a visual reminder to help all of you stay focused on your values and the things you're committed to. The values you pass on to your kids will help them prioritize their spending and set meaningful and compelling goals for themselves. The combination of solid values and strong money management skills creates a good foundation for making sound financial and life decisions.

THE TEN HEALTHY HABITS OF FINANCIAL MANAGEMENT

As we have indicated, becoming a money-smart family starts with developing healthy financial habits and then modelling them for your kids.

Throughout this guide, we will refer to the Taylor family, Robert, Michelle and their daughter Emma, as a great example of how to do things right. They have 10 healthy habits for managing their finances — simple, common-sense guidelines that keep their affairs in order and set the stage for any discussions they may want to have with their kid about money. Here they are:

1. **Know where you stand financially**

    The starting point for the Taylors was figuring out their net worth: everything they own less everything they owe. And they keep a close eye on it, making sure it's moving in the right direction, with assets growing and debt shrinking. Why not take the first step in figuring out where you stand by completing the Net Worth Worksheet at the end of this chapter.

The Taylors also know how much money comes in every month (and every year). They understand that it is a finite amount, and they treat it with care. Equally important, they understand that managing money is about making choices. Like the rest of us, they have to decide what to do with the money that comes in: how much to save, spend, share and invest. And they control how much money goes out by monitoring their household cash flow, using a template similar to our Cash Flow Calculator at the end of this chapter.

2. **Live within your means**

Arguably, this is the most important lesson you can teach your kids. And the best way to teach it is to actually live this way, to walk the walk. The Taylors simply do not spend more than they make. In fact, they make sure they can't spend more than they make because they always follow the third healthy habit.

3. **Save/Pay yourself first**

Every month, they take a certain amount of money directly from their pay cheques and put it into savings. To make it really easy, they set it up as an automatic transfer. They've gotten used to living without this money and they spend only what remains. They don't rack up credit card debt or balances on home equity loans or lines of credit because they follow the fourth healthy habit.

4. **Understand the difference between good debt and bad debt**

The Taylors understand that credit can be a wonderful tool when used responsibly. Credit is convenient—much more convenient than using cash or cheques. Credit can also act as a safety net in case of an emergency (more on that in healthy habit #5). Building a good credit history enables you to make big purchases such as a car or a house at a reasonable interest rate and, like many families, the Taylors have a mortgage on their house. Incurring debt for the purpose of buying an asset—something that adds to your net worth and has the potential to go up in value, such as a house or a stock—is an example of "good debt". Student loan debt is another example of "good debt", as it is an investment in the student's future career and earning power.

However, even with good debt you must never take on more than you can repay within a reasonable period of time. If you have trouble servicing your debt (you pay late or you miss payments), you will damage your credit rating. Bad credit hurts: you may be denied loans or have to pay extremely high interest rates, and you may face higher insurance rates. Some employers are even checking the credit of prospective employees. They see credit history as an indication of responsibility.

"Bad Debt", which is something the Taylors actively avoid, is debt incurred to purchase consumption goods such as furniture, appliances, TVs and clothes. These items have almost no resale value, do not go up in value (in fact they lose value the minute you walk out of the store with them) and do not add to your net worth. Going into debt on your credit card or department store card to buy these types of items is very costly by the time you factor in the interest expense. The Taylors save up for these types of purchases.

5. **Set up a financial safety net**

The Taylors want their family to be protected in case a financial emergency occurs. A rule of thumb is to have three to six months' worth of living expenses in cash reserves because if you become unemployed, that is how long it takes, on average, to find a new job in your field. They opted for the more prudent larger amount. This will enable them to keep up their mortgage payments and buy food if one of them suddenly loses their job. They also have adequate life and disability insurance, as well as automobile and homeowner's insurance.

FAMILY DISCUSSION
Needs vs. Wants

Before deciding to make a purchase, ask your kid to answer this question:

"Do I really need this, or would it just be nice to have?"

You'd be amazed at how much money that simple question can save you! And you might be surprised at your kids' willingness to give it a try.

6. **Know the difference between needs and wants**

If you want something badly enough, it can be really easy to convince yourself you need it, especially given the very powerful forces in the media that try to convince us that our wants actually are needs. Our kids are bombarded at least as much as we are, if not more, and they may lack the critical thinking skills that might help us deconstruct the advertisers' methods and messages. We're not doing our kids—or ourselves—any favours by giving in to their every demand.

7. **Teach delayed gratification and set financial goals**

Delaying gratification is another important life skill you can help your kids develop. A famous psychological study, called the "Marshmallow Test", proved this. It showed the effect of impulse control and willpower on academic, emotional and social success.

A group of 4-year-olds were given marshmallows. They were told that they could have one marshmallow now, but if they could wait several minutes, they could have two. Some children grabbed a marshmallow and ate it. Others waited, some covering their eyes to avoid seeing the tempting treat. One child even licked the table around the marshmallow!

Over 14 years, the researchers followed the group and found that the "grabbers" suffered low self-esteem and were perceived by others as prone to envy and easily frustrated. The "waiters" coped better and were more socially competent and self-assertive, trustworthy, dependable and more academically successful. The lesson: strong willpower and impulse control will help us stay on task and meet our goals throughout our lives, whether it's studying instead of watching TV or saving for retirement instead of spending.

Setting financial goals is one thing you can do that helps teach delayed gratification. And setting goals can be easy.

Just writing them down and being able to see a list or a collage takes away some of the urgency around buying them. Waiting for a reward by setting goals in this way — and delaying gratification — also helps to counter any attitude of entitlement your kids may have picked up. Many parents also find they can delay gratification on "big ticket" items by connecting them to a special occasion like a birthday, Christmas or other holiday.

> **THINGS TO DO**
> *Wish list*
>
> Create a "wish list" of wants with your kids. It can take many forms:
>
> - Make a simple, written list.
>
> - Create a "vision board" or collage of images of things your kids want.

Sometimes, kids just need reminding that shiny new things lose their lustre pretty quickly. When Emma Taylor was young and was pestering her parents for something she just "had to have", Michelle used to ask her: "Remember the last thing you had to have? What was that again? And do you have any idea where it is?" It was usually somewhere in the corner of their basement play-room gathering dust!

8. **Track your spending**

There are many different ways to track your spending. It doesn't matter how you do it, the important thing is that you bring awareness to your spending habits. It's a great reality check. You may be shocked to learn that your actual spending bears very little resemblance to how you think you spend your money. You may also find that writing everything down is a powerful motivator to make better spending choices.

THINGS TO DO
Tracking spending

Which of the following would work best for you?

- Keep a written spending journal
- Use a spreadsheet
- Download your banking data directly to financial software, or
- Use a smartphone app.

If tracking all of your spending seems overwhelming, there is a shortcut you can take. Start with your "problem areas". We all have them—those little indulgences that are more want than need. It could be your daily latte habit, or a weakness for the latest electronic devices. Begin by just tracking those.

The Taylors also take the extra step of comparing their actual spending to their budget to see if they're on track. Because a budget is a work in progress, the Taylors use what they learn to tweak their budget on a regular basis and make it more realistic.

9. **Save now for your children's education**

The Taylors have done this right. They take full advantage of tax-assisted programs offered by the government to help save for their kids' post-secondary education. The government created the **Registered Education Savings Plan (RESP)** for this purpose. Although the amounts you put into an RESP are not tax deductible—that is, you must first pay any tax due on the money you contribute   you do not pay tax on any gains or investment income you earn while the funds remain in the plan.

The other major benefit of saving money in an RESP is that the government will also contribute funds into the plan; their contribution is called a Canada

Education Savings Grant (CESG). The amount of the grant is 20% of contributions, to a maximum of $500 per child per year, and a lifetime limit of $7,200. See Resources at the end of the book for further resources related to RESPs.

Earnings accumulated in the RESP, as well as government grants, must be used to pay for the cost of post-secondary education. These amounts are taxable income to the student in the year paid out (they can use other tax credits available to students to offset tax they would otherwise owe). The original contributions can be paid out to the student or parent tax-free.

10. **Present a united money front**

It complicates matters when parents do not agree on important issues. This is especially true when it comes to money, which is why disagreement over money issues is one of the leading causes of divorce. But it's really important for parents to present a united money front. If your kids sense an opportunity to get what they want by exploiting the fact that their parents are not on the same page, they will take full advantage. As we've seen, values influence your financial behaviour, and it's best if you and your partner can arrive at shared values. In addition to showing your kids that it is possible to discuss and come to agreement about money, it also makes it much easier to set financial goals for your family.

Managing finances responsibly can seem like a daunting task. Maybe you're already doing it well. If so, congratulations! If not, though, we hope some of the information and resources in this chapter will help you get your own financial matters in order. And the following chapters should help you talk about money management with your kids in a way that they can relate to at different stages of their young lives.

KEY POINTS

- As a parent, you are a role model for your kids—probably their most important role model. This is just as true in money matters as in other important aspects of life. The best way to raise money-smart kids is to be smart about money yourself ... and to talk to them about how money works.

- Kids who learn lessons about money management from a young age have a better chance of becoming healthy, happy and successful adults who are financially responsible and independent.

- 10 Healthy Habits of Financial Management:
  1. Know where you stand financially
  2. Live within your means
  3. Save/Pay yourself first
  4. Understand the difference between good debt and bad debt
  5. Set up a financial safety net
  6. Know the difference between needs and wants
  7. Teach delayed gratification and set financial goals
  8. Track your spending
  9. Save now for your children's education
  10. Present a united money front.

Resources

ROLE MODEL SELF-ASSESSMENT[1]

Answer these statements with either True or False.	True or False
1. I would not stretch myself financially in order to drive a nice car	
2. I try to stay up to date on the tax issues that affect me	
3. I like to discuss investments	
4. If I won the lottery, I would not noticeably change my lifestyle	
5. I am usually eager to get to work	
6. Learning is an important key to financial success	
7. I am reasonably careful with money	
8. I adhere to a structured budget	
9. I always conduct due diligence on my investments	
10. When I get advice, I seek a second opinion	
11. I keep well informed for everyday financial decisions	
12. I know where I am going and how to get there	
13. If there is something I "want" but don't "need", I walk away and sleep on it	
14. I pay off my credit card balance every month	
15. I reflect on my past investment decisions to see what I can learn	
16. I do not "gamble" with my savings by taking excess risk	
17. I try to shop carefully, using coupons and waiting for sales	
18. I can afford everything I need	

Less than 10 Trues: You have some work to do!

10–15 Trues: You are modelling good behaviour some of the time. Keep working on it!

15–18 Trues: Congratulations, you are modelling good behaviour almost all the time!

1   Inspired by Financial Attitudes Exercise in *Client-Centered Life Planning*, Michael R. Curtis (Toronto, Canada: Michael R. Curtis, 2005).

Resources

CASH FLOW CALCULATOR[2]

Create a Budget—Manage Your Debt Effectively

Use this tool to help give you a clear picture of your cash flow. You'll be able to determine how much debt you can comfortably afford in order to achieve your goals.

MONTHLY INCOME	
Salary after taxes (take-home pay, Self-employment/Business income)	$
Other income (e.g. investment income)	$
Total Income	$

MONTHLY EXPENSES—FIXED	
Housing Costs (e.g. mortgage, rent, condo/maintenance fees, property taxes, etc.)	$
Utilities—Heat, hydro, water	$
Services—Phone, home and mobile, cable/satellite, internet, security system	$
Insurance—Auto, home, life, disability	$
Child care	$
Existing Loans and credit cards (minimum monthly payments)	$
Other fixed expenses (e.g. child support, alimony, etc)	$
Total Expenses—Fixed	$

...continued

2   www.rbcroyalbank.com/products/personalloans/budget/budget-calculator.html

Resources

CASH FLOW CALCULATOR (continued)

MONTHLY EXPENSES—VARIABLE	
Groceries	$
Household Maintenance (e.g. renovations, landscaping and gardening, house cleaning, snow removal, lawn care, etc.)	$
Transportation (e.g. car lease, gas, transit, car service & repairs, parking fees, licence & registration, etc.)	$
Uninsured health services (e.g. prescriptions, dental care, eye care, counseling, any other health services not covered under a plan)	$
Education (e.g. tuition, books, exam fees, etc)	$
Long term Savings (e.g. monthly pension plan, RSP, education saving contribution)	$
Other Variable Expenses	$
Total Expenses—Variable	$

MONTHLY EXPENSES—DISCRETIONARY	
Personal (e.g. clothing, shoes, gifts, salon, gym membership, etc.)	$
Daily living (e.g. pet expenses, dry cleaning, etc.)	$
Entertainment (e.g. dining out, movies, music, theatre/concerts etc.)	$
Donations	$
Vacation	$
Other Discretionary Expenses	$
Total Expenses—Discretionary	$

Resources

RRSP NET WORTH WORKSHEET[3]

RRSP Net Worth Worksheet

1. Assets and Liabilities

Use this handy financial worksheet for a "snapshot" of what you own (your assets) and what you owe (your liabilities).

ASSETS AND LIABILITIES	
Assets (what you own)	
Non registered assets	
Chequing/savings account(s):	$
GICs/term deposits:	$
Canada Savings Bonds:	$
Stocks, bonds, mutual funds:	$
Investment properties:	$
Cash value of life insurance:	$
Home(s):	$
Automobile(s):	$
Boat(s):	$
	$
	$
	$

...continued

3   www.rbcroyalbank.com/cgi-bin/retirement/networth/start.cgi

Resources

RRSP NET WORTH WORKSHEET (continued)

1. Assets and Liabilities (continued)

REGISTERED ASSETS	
RRSPs, DPSPs, RRIFs:	$
Locked-in RRSPs, LIRAs, LIFs, LRIFs:	$
Value of pension plan(s):	$
Other (e.g. annuities):	$
	$
	$
	$

LIABILITIES (WHAT YOU OWE)	
Mortgage(s):[4]	$
Income/property taxes owing:	$
Car loan/lease:[5]	$
Credit card balance(s):	$
Personal line of credit:	
Other loans:	
Other debts:	
Unpaid bills:	

...continued

4   Outstanding principal on mortgage(s)

5   Outstanding principal on car loan or total outstanding leasing obligation

Resources

RRSP NET WORTH WORKSHEET (continued)

1. Assets and Liabilities (continued)

LIABILITIES (WHAT YOU OWE) (continued)	
Other obligations:[6]	$
	$
	$
	$

Note: Record the value of all assets and liabilities, putting a realistic market value on tangible assets such as property, car(s), etc.

2. Net Worth

ASSETS AND LIABILITIES	
Total Assets	$
Total Liabilities	$
Net Worth	$

...continued

6   Annual amount of other obligations including daycare, alimony payments, etc.

Resources

VALUES VALIDATOR[7]

Helping you discover what is really important to you

Use this method of ranking:

Not important	0
Somewhat important	1–3
Quite important	4–7
Very important	8–10

	VALUE	DESCRIPTION	RATING (OUT OF 10)
1	Academics	I have high regard for scholastic pursuits.	
2	Achievement	It's important to accomplish my goals.	
3	Activity	I like to be fully occupied at all times.	
4	Advancement	I want the opportunity for career advancement.	
5	Adventure	I like to do things in new and interesting ways.	
6	Enjoyment	I want to enjoy life and have fun.	
7	Expertise	I want to be a known authority in my field.	
8	Family	I want to contribute to family members.	
9	Friendship	I want close companionship.	
10	Health	I want to be healthy and pursue a healthy lifestyle.	
11	Independence	I like to be able to work or be alone and free from constraints.	
12	Location	I want to be able to live anywhere.	

7   Adapted from Values worksheet in Financial Attitudes Exercise in Client-Centered Life Planning, Michael R. Curtis (Toronto, Canada: Michael R. Curtis, 2005).

Resources

VALUES VALIDATOR (continued)

	VALUE	DESCRIPTION	RATING (OUT OF 10)
13	Power	I want to have influence over my future.	
14	Prestige	I like to obtain recognition and status.	
15	Routine	I like to have a set daily schedule.	
16	Security	I like to minimize adverse changes in my life.	
17	Self-Development	I want to be the best that I can be.	
18	Self-Realization	I like to realize the full potential of my skills and abilities.	
19	Social Service	I want to serve others.	
20	Wealth	I want to be able to afford opportunities.	

Rank your top 5 values

...continued

CHAPTER

2

"Mommy, I know money doesn't grow on trees—it comes from the bank machine!"

Teaching Young Children

GUIDELINES FOR CHILDREN 5 TO 8 YEARS OLD

Kids become familiar with money at a very early age because they see us use it daily. In most families, teaching kids about money begins when they start asking about it and when they start asking for things! This usually begins to happen around the time a child starts pre-school or elementary school. For instance, your kid may see the toys, books, and clothing that other kids have and begin asking for specific items or even brands. Or your child may simply express curiosity about money; the way it looks, the different colours on our paper bills and the different sizes and shapes of the coins we use.

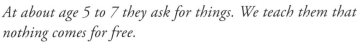

At about age 5 to 7 they ask for things. We teach them that nothing comes for free.

EARN

WHAT IS MONEY?

Bills and coins

At this age, you can let your kids handle money and start to develop an understanding of Canadian currency; show them the different coins and bills and talk to them about what they're worth. You can point out the different images

on the "heads" and "tails" sides of the coins and discuss how each of them is a very special and important image of Canada: the maple leaf, the beaver, the moose, the loon and the polar bear, to name a few. Point out the different dates on each coin and see if your kids can find a coin from the year they were born. You can also tell your kids that our coins are made by the Royal Canadian Mint (**www.mint.ca**) and discuss what metal the coins are made of (copper for pennies; nickel for nickels, dimes and quarters; bronze for loonies; and nickel and bronze for toonies). In addition to everyday coins, show them special coins like 50 cent pieces and silver dollars or commemorative coins like the Terry Fox loonie or the poppy quarter.

There are lots of facts about money that your kids may find interesting at this age and as they get older. They may be surprised to learn that although our bills look like "paper" money, they are actually made out of 100% cotton—just like their t-shirts—but much stronger! Our colourful bills are printed by the Bank of Canada and have special markings and security features on them to prevent people from making counterfeit or fake money. Discussing who appears on the bills (and coins) can also be a history, not just a math, lesson! You can check out the Bank of Canada website for money matters that might intrigue your kids: (**www.bankofcanada.ca/en/ banknotes/index.html**). And if your kids are really interested in money, you may want to visit the currency museum website, especially the resources in the Learning Centre at **www.currencymuseum.ca**.

Generally, young children are able to count to 10 and have a basic knowledge of numbers and quantities. To teach them what money is worth, you can make it fun by playing games.

For more games and activities that you can play with your kids, please visit the website of the Office of the Superintendent of Bankruptcy Canada at **www.ic.gc.ca/eic/site/bsf-osb.nsf/eng/br01618. html#toc1**.

Barter

Your kids may be curious about why we use money to buy things. They may ask you how bills and coins became the way to pay for things. If your kids are at the upper end of the age range, you may want to start by explaining that money replaced the barter system. Centuries ago, it was much harder for people to get what they needed. Instead of using coins and currency, all they had to offer as payment

THINGS TO DO
Games with coins

Help your kid to sort a jar of coins into different piles.

- Count out five pennies and then ask her for one nickel, explaining that a nickel is worth five cents.

- Ask your kid to count out an additional five pennies plus the nickel she just got and exchange it for one dime and explain that a dime is worth ten cents and that it is worth twice as much as a nickel.

- Give your kid a quarter, explaining that it is worth 25 cents and more valuable than a penny, nickel or dime.

As she gets older, the games can become a bit more challenging:

- Ask her what combination of nickels and dimes she'd have to give in exchange for a quarter.

- Move on to the loonie and the toonie, which are especially appealing to her because of their size, shape and colour (and their relative value).

- Describe the loonie as being worth 100 cents or one dollar and challenge your kid to find different combinations of pennies, nickels, dimes or quarters that would add up to one loonie.

- Ask if she can guess what the toonie is worth, based on the sound of its name!

was goods or services in exchange for whatever the other person had. This is called barter. For example, if you were a grape grower, you could exchange your grapes for the potato farmer's potatoes. Or you could hire workers to help you with the harvest and pay them in grapes. But because grapes were all you had to exchange, if you needed a chicken and the chicken farmer didn't want or need grapes, you would not be able to get any chicken. As a result, most societies realized that they needed something that everyone agreed had value and could be used to pay for things — money.

In the earliest days, money was made out of whatever was rare or highly desired, like beads, whale teeth, feathers and even huge stone discs carved out of limestone! Slowly, almost every country switched to a much more convenient system of bills and coins backed by the government.

Foreign currencies

Your kids may be interested in currency from other countries because it looks so different from Canadian money. For example, you may want to show your child an American $1 or $5 bill. Unlike our bills, American bills are all the same green colour and as a result they're a little harder to tell apart. Also, coins from foreign countries can be interesting to young kids, especially ones that have holes in the centre and ones that are made from different materials and feel different than our coins.

The value of a dollar

Every parent says they want their kids to know and appreciate the value of a dollar. But young kids are not very worldly, so it's harder for them to appreciate what things cost. The challenge is to explain relative value by using examples they can relate to, like toys or food. You can show them that one apple costs one loonie but **one** ice cream cone costs **two** loonies, so an ice cream cone is worth twice as much (or is twice as expensive) as an apple. If a toy that they want costs $20, you can show them that you'd have to pay for it with **twenty** loonies which means it's worth twenty times more than an apple and ten times

FAMILY DISCUSSION
Foreign currency

Explain to your kids that when you travel to another country, you cannot use your Canadian money. You have to exchange Canadian money for the local currency. Not all countries use dollars—some use yen or euros. And just because another country's bill says $1, it doesn't mean that it's worth the same as our $1 coin! We may have to pay more than $1, say $1.20, to buy a single unit of another currency.

more than an ice cream cone. We will discuss more opportunities to teach young kids the valuc of a dollar later in this chapter under "Teachable Moments".

We started with coins. What does a quarter buy? Four quarters equals one dollar; what does one dollar buy? You can teach what things cost that way and go on to percents and interest and return on investment.

WHERE DOES MONEY COME FROM?
(NO, THE ANSWER IS NOT THE ATM MACHINE!)

When I tell my 7-year-old daughter that I don't have any more money for toys or candy, she tells me to go to the ATM machine!

Funny, but it also reminds us that young kids may not always understand where money comes from. They may think it actually does grow on trees or comes from a magic machine that spits out bills. They are probably too young to appreciate what making a living is all about, and how hard you have to work to earn money. But they can understand that when you leave in the morning, you are going to work, doing whatever it is you do, in order to make money for the family.

You can explain to them that the money you make gets deposited into your bank account, which is connected to the bank machine. The money you withdraw pays for food, clothes, the car—all the things at home that they can see and touch. It also pays for some things they can't see, like the mortgage on the house or rent on the apartment where you live, heat and air conditioning, electricity and the Internet! You can also explain that you are able to buy them things they want, like toys or candy, in addition to things they need, and what the difference is. They are not too young to be grateful for what they have and to know that there are others who are less fortunate.

FAMILY DISCUSSION
Jobs

- Ask your kids to name some other jobs they see people do, e.g., teacher, dentist, eye doctor, garbage collector, mailman.

- Ask them what kind of education they might need to do that job. Discuss the connection between education, jobs/careers and making money.

" *My son understands that you need to work to earn money to live. He is aware of the fact that his mom and dad work in order to buy him his favourite food or toy. He often says to me that he wants to work on his computer to make money, because he sees his mom and dad working on their computers. It is never too early to start. He even pretends to use a plastic card as his credit card!*

"Mommy, I know money doesn't grow on trees–it comes from the bank machine!"

Because young kids love pushing the buttons of the ATM machine, take them with you next time you make a deposit or a withdrawal. Tell them to think of the ATM machine as a giant piggy bank; you can put money in or take money out. But if you don't make any money, you have nothing to deposit and the bank card is useless because there is no money to withdraw. You may also consider showing your child your online bank statement; the money you deposit is added to your account and the money you withdraw is deducted. When you punch in your PIN, explain that this secret code makes sure that only you can deposit or withdraw money to and from your account and that it must be guarded carefully.

BIRTHDAY AND TOOTH FAIRY MONEY

There are special occasions when young kids "earn" or receive money. Your kids may get money from the "tooth fairy" when they lose their baby teeth, and/or money from friends and family on their birthdays or on significant holidays like Christmas or Chanukah. These are important opportunities to introduce them to the concept that when you **EARN** money, you have money choices: **SAVE**, **SPEND**, **SHARE** and **INVEST**. It's important to choose well, because once the money is spent, it's no longer available for other things.

My son was saving up to buy Silly Bandz, those rubber bracelets in the shape of different animals that were the hottest fad. All the kids were collecting and trading them. When he finally had enough money, he ran to the store, bought the Silly Bandz, piled them on his wrist and ran over to his friend's house to trade. But his friend, and all the other kids, had already moved on to the next fad and were no longer interested in Silly Bandz. Suddenly, neither was my son. He no longer had any money but he learned two important lessons: when it's gone, it's gone, and don't fall for every fad!

ALLOWANCE: PAYMENT FOR CHORES, A MONEY MANAGEMENT TOOL, OR BOTH?

Allowance has become a controversial topic among parents and financial experts. But it never used to be. When I was growing up, you got an allowance for doing some basic chores around the house. If you didn't do them, your parents held back on your allowance. Back then, no one thought of allowance as a money management tool. Parents didn't consider that by withholding their kid's allowance, they were depriving them of the opportunity to learn how to manage money when the stakes were low.

FAMILY DISCUSSION
Allowance

What is your philosophy about allowance?

a) Payment for chores

b) Payment for good grades

c) A money management tool

d) All of the above

Some parents firmly believe that their kids need to "earn" their allowance, either by doing household chores or perhaps by getting good grades (more on that in Chapter 3). They believe that this establishes a connection between putting forth an effort and earning money. Others believe just as strongly that their kids should help out around the house without getting paid because it is their responsibility as a member of the family to contribute. They believe that paying them sends the wrong message: that they should expect compensation for everything they do. There is no right or wrong answer. As always, you have to do what works for your child and your family.

When do I start and how much do I give?

For young kids, one rule of thumb is to base their allowance on their age. A 5-year-old would get $5 a week and a 7-year-old would get $7. It's simple and makes sense to kids. Another strategy is to estimate what your child reasonably spends in a week (say $3 on treats) and then add a little more for savings, sharing and investing. You also have to decide what's affordable for your family. Pay allowance on a regular basis so that it feels like a steady income your kids can rely on.

Limitations or laissez-faire?

Because of their age and level of maturity, young children need more guidance when it comes to money choices than older children. Although they may already be consumers, at this age they do not have a realistic attitude about money. As the Marshmallow Test in Chapter 1 taught us, some have not yet developed self-discipline and impulse control. They need training and they respond well to a parent or teacher who is willing to teach financial concepts in a fun way.

SAVE

In Chapter 1 we talked about the importance of delayed gratification, setting goals and saving. Saving is basically deferred spending. When it comes to saving, almost any toy or item your child wants can become a goal. The next time your child asks for a certain toy or game, suggest that he use his allowance to save for it. Once enough money has been saved up, take him to the store to make the big purchase!

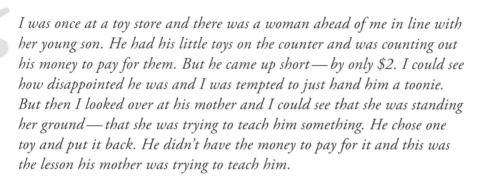

I was once at a toy store and there was a woman ahead of me in line with her young son. He had his little toys on the counter and was counting out his money to pay for them. But he came up short — by only $2. I could see how disappointed he was and I was tempted to just hand him a toonie. But then I looked over at his mother and I could see that she was standing her ground — that she was trying to teach him something. He chose one toy and put it back. He didn't have the money to pay for it and this was the lesson his mother was trying to teach him.

Although the woman taught her son a valuable lesson, you have to be careful not to discourage your kids from reaching their goals, especially if it's their first attempt at saving. One way to effectively encourage your kids towards a goal is to offer to match their savings. If your child agrees to save $5 towards a $10 toy, you can offer to match their savings with an additional $5.

MULTI-SLOTTED PIGGY BANKS

Piggy banks are an old-fashioned way to teach young kids to save, and are still popular today.

But piggy banks have come a long way — we now have multi-slotted piggy banks. They have a built-in feature to help young kids make smart and deliberate money choices: separate slots and compartments for save, spend, share and invest! (See **www.msgen.com/assembled/money_savvy_pig.html**.)

Using their allowance, birthday or tooth fairy money, your child can decide how much to allocate to each category. Remember to give them their allowance in different denominations to make it easier for them to make the allocations.

I like the kind of piggy bank that you can't open, that you literally have to break open with a hammer when it gets full. Otherwise, if you can open it, it's too tempting to borrow or steal from your savings and the next thing you know the piggy bank is empty!

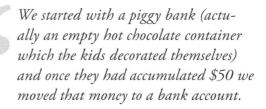

We started with a piggy bank (actually an empty hot chocolate container which the kids decorated themselves) and once they had accumulated $50 we moved that money to a bank account.

FAMILY DISCUSSION
Piggy banks

What kind of piggy bank would work for your kid?

a) A piggy bank that can be opened

b) A multi-slotted piggy bank

c) A vault—"My kid has no willpower!"

SPEND

TEACHABLE MOMENTS

Since young kids are often with you when they are out in the world, opportunities abound to teach them about money. You don't have to set aside extra time. These opportunities will occur organically in your everyday lives. Think of them as "teachable moments".

You have a lot of influence over your kids at this age. Although they are also influenced by siblings, peers and the media, they place the most confidence in what you, their parents, say. And as parents, you know what's appropriate for your own kids, so take advantage of situations as they arise to teach them to make smart choices.

At the grocery or corner store

Every transaction at the store is a chance to teach your kids about money. When the storekeeper gives you your total, ask your child to help you count out the money you owe. Then have her pay for the items and count the change she gets back, making sure it's the right amount. Teach her to get a receipt, in case a mistake is made and you have to return something.

"May I have a receipt please?"

At the mall

You've already explained how the ATM works. Next time you're at the mall and you use your debit card to buy something, show your kids that it's the same card you use to deposit and withdraw money at the ATM. Explain that using a bank card in a store means that the cost of whatever you buy comes out of your bank account right away. Show them that you punch in the same secret code at the store as at the ATM machine. Remind them that the secret code means that only you can buy things and pay for them with the money in your account.

At the restaurant

Next time you take your kids out to dinner and you pay using your credit card, take the time to teach them what a credit card is and how it works. Explain to them that unlike paying with cash or your debit card, when you pay with your credit card the money does not come out of your bank account right away. Instead, you are allowed to pay later, when the credit card bill is due.

Planning a birthday party

Children's birthdays provide opportunities to teach valuable money lessons, as we will see here and under "Share" below. Involving your kids in planning their birthday parties can introduce them to the idea of budgeting in a fun way.

For Emma Taylor's 8th birthday, she really wanted to have a movie party. The latest Harry Potter movie had just come out and she and all her friends couldn't wait to see it. She spoke to her parents about the idea and they said yes, as long as Emma agreed to help plan it. Michelle and Robert realized that planning the party could be a teachable moment. They sat down with Emma to talk about all the different costs: the cost of a child's movie ticket, the cost of a few adult movie tickets (for the chaperones), the cost of snacks like popcorn, candy and drinks, and the cost of an ice cream cake for the party after.

Emma had a great idea that would save money and paper: use e-vites. Her parents loved that! They discussed an overall budget for the party and Robert explained to Emma that the more kids she invited, the more the party would cost. So Emma thought really hard and invited only her close friends, in order to keep the cost of the party within her budget.

FAMILY DISCUSSION
Credit cards

- Show your kids your credit card statement so they can see the amounts and entries on the statement.

- Point out the purchases that were made for them, or dinners you ate together in restaurants.

- Show them how all of the credit card purchases add up to one big amount that you have to pay with money in your bank account.

- Explain that if you don't have the money in your bank account, you will be charged interest, which means that the amount you owe keeps getting bigger.

FAMILY DISCUSSION
Teachable moments

What other teachable moments can you find in your daily lives?

Board games

Board games, and especially games that teach money lessons, are popular.

In the Taylor house they love playing games like Monopoly, where the object of the game is to become the wealthiest player through buying, renting and selling property. They also like playing the game of Life. This game simulates a person's travels through his or her life, from college to retirement, with jobs, marriages and possibly children along the way.

SHARE

GET A GIFT/GIVE A GIFT

Birthday parties are a really big deal for young kids. It's something they look forward to all year—having fun with their friends, eating cake and getting presents!

On Emma Taylor's 7th birthday, Robert and Michelle let her invite all the kids in her class to her party, but they really didn't think Emma needed 20 gifts. They felt that her birthday could be an opportunity to teach her about sharing. So Michelle decided that they would ask half of the guests to make a donation in honour of Emma's birthday instead of buying a gift. She let Emma choose the charity and Emma chose Birthday Angels. (Birthday Angels organizes birthday parties for children at risk, some of whom have never had a birthday party in their lives.)

The remaining guests pooled their money and bought Emma one very special gift that had been on Emma's birthday "wish list". Emma was really excited to receive the gift she had been wanting for so long, but she was also really happy that some of her gifts went to helping other kids celebrate and enjoy their birthdays. The Taylors were thrilled that Emma wanted to share her birthday with other kids. They were also happy for Emma to have a tangible example of delayed gratification: the special birthday gift that had been on her "wish list" all year.

> **FAMILY DISCUSSION**
> *Charity*
>
> Is donating birthday gifts to charity something your family would do?
>
> a) No, my son would want all the gifts
>
> b) Yes, half going to charity and half to my child feels right
>
> c) Yes, but we would ask that all gifts be donated to charity

DONATING CHANGE FOR A CHARITY — IT ADDS UP!

The Taylor family loved going to Tim Hortons. And not just for the coffee and Timbits®, but also for the opportunities it presented for teachable moments. Michelle would always ask Emma to count out the money they owed as well as the change she received. Michelle remembers one trip to Tim's, where they went through their usual routine of Emma paying and getting their change, but this time Emma asked her mom if she could throw the coins in the charity box beside the cash register, because she noticed that they were raising money to send kids to camp. She loved going to camp and wanted other kids to have that experience too. Emma started to think about all of the customers that came in and out of that one Tim's, every hour, all day long. And she started to think about how if everyone donated just a little bit of change, even 25 cents each, it could really add up.

INVEST

ENCOURAGING ENTREPRENEURSHIP — BEYOND THE "LEMONADE STAND"

Emma Taylor was always very enterprising, even as a young kid. When all the other little kids on her street set up lemonade stands, Emma decided she wanted to do something just a little bit different. She had always enjoyed art at school and even took an extra-curricular art program at a local art school. She was quite prolific—all the different pieces she had created were really starting to accumulate. So Emma decided to create an art gallery in her parents' living room to showcase her art. She invited all of her friends, their parents, her family and neighbours to view and buy pieces of her art. She priced each piece based on the amount of time it took her to create them, and what she thought people would pay for them. She sent out e-vites and bought some refreshments to serve during the show.

The show was a big success! Many "art patrons" bought pieces of Emma's art, and with each sale Emma recorded the name of the piece and the amount it sold for in a notebook. She also made sure to give each customer a receipt. At the end of the show, Emma added up all the sales she had recorded in her notebook to determine her gross sales. Then she deducted the cost of the refreshments she had served. Emma turned a nice profit! She paid herself first by allocating some to savings, set aside some proceeds for donating and spending, and invested the rest — on more art supplies for her growing business!

KEY POINTS

- Kids are curious. They spend a lot of time just trying to figure out how the world works. If they're old enough to ask questions about money, then they're old enough to deserve a good answer.

- You don't have to schedule a family conference to have great conversations with your kid about money. The opportunity will present itself countless times in your everyday life. The trick is to recognize those "teachable moments" and to take advantage of them.

- Teaching kids about money can be fun for them and for you. Capitalize on this fun factor when you talk to your kid about money — education can have a big element of entertainment at this age.

CHAPTER

3

Teaching Pre-Teens

GUIDELINES FOR PRE-TEENS 9 TO 12 YEARS OLD

As your kids become a little older, you will be noticing many changes. Hopefully they're a little more responsible and mature, and certainly at this age they have a better grasp of math. Perhaps they're more interested in money now than when they were younger. But just like younger kids, pre-teens have money choices, and as parents it's your job to give them the right tools and knowledge to make sensible ones.

EARN

JOBS: BABYSITTING, DOG WALKING, CAR WASHING AND OTHER ODD JOBS

Because your pre-teen is also a little more independent, they have the opportunity to earn money by working "odd jobs". A job can make them more responsible. For many pre-teens, their first job is babysitting. Schools often offer babysitting training and "certification" for kids in Grade 6 or 7. So encourage your kids to find babysitting gigs, either for extended family, friends or neighbours.

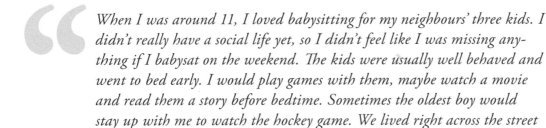

When I was around 11, I loved babysitting for my neighbours' three kids. I didn't really have a social life yet, so I didn't feel like I was missing anything if I babysat on the weekend. The kids were usually well behaved and went to bed early. I would play games with them, maybe watch a movie and read them a story before bedtime. Sometimes the oldest boy would stay up with me to watch the hockey game. We lived right across the street so I knew I could call my mom to help me if there was a problem. And they always had the best snacks! Looking back, it was probably the easiest money I ever made.

Other jobs that are also suitable for your pre-teen include dog walking or pet sitting, snow shovelling, car washing or grass cutting. Encourage them to be creative when looking to make extra money. If they're technically inclined, perhaps they can tutor a grown-up on computer or smartphone use. Or, if they're strong academically, maybe they can tutor younger students in reading or math.

These jobs are likely to pay differently. The going rate for an hour of babysitting may be less than what they can make washing a car for an hour. If your pre-teen is trying to save up for something specific in a very short period of time, he may look for jobs with the highest pay.

At this age, if they like what they're doing they are more likely to stick with it. They will get to experience the satisfaction of doing something they love and doing it well—and getting paid for it! As they get older and start thinking about career choices this will be an important message: when you are passionate about what you do, it doesn't feel like "work".

ALLOWANCE REVISITED: PAYMENT FOR CHORES, A MONEY MANAGEMENT TOOL OR BOTH?

As highlighted in Chapter 2, different parents have different philosophies about allowance. Some see it as payment for chores, some see it as a way to teach their kids money management skills, and some see it as both. Usually when kids are in their pre-teen years their allowance increases and therefore the stakes get higher about how they use it. What's important is that you are clear with your kid about what your philosophy is, and that your kid understands why she's getting an allowance and why it is the amount it is … and what her responsibilities are regarding how the money will be used.

Know what motivates your kid

What motivates your pre-teen? Is she motivated by extrinsic rewards like money? (There's nothing wrong with that—we're all motivated to varying degrees by money.) If that's the case, paying her to do her assigned chores will ensure they get done and will give her some money to manage. But if she doesn't do her chores, do you take away her allowance? Often as parents, we do this as a knee-jerk reaction because it feels like the only leverage we have. But we're probably better off letting our kids get their allowance so they can continue to practise managing money. There are plenty of other consequences that can be meted out for not doing chores—like less time on the computer or the Xbox!

> *When my daughter doesn't do her chores, rather than take away her allowance, I take away access to the computer and video games—things I don't want her spending so much time on anyway!*

But maybe your kid is intrinsically motivated. Does he have the drive and discipline to do his chores or his homework without connecting it to his allowance? If that's the case, then his allowance can be given as a pure money management tool.

Finally, you can always give your kids opportunities to earn extra money by doing things around the house that go above and beyond their normal responsibilities.

> *My kids were always looking for opportunities to earn a little extra money. So I told them that if I had to hire and pay someone to do something, like mow the lawn, shovel snow or rake leaves, then I would be happy to pay them instead. But taking out the garbage did not count —I certainly wasn't going to hire anyone outside the family to do that!*

How much allowance to give?

The age formula that you used to decide how much allowance to give when your kids were younger is probably no longer appropriate. At this stage, their allowance should be based on a budget.

> *When my son turned 11, he asked for a raise in his allowance. I told him that if he wanted to get more money, he had to take a course about money that his school was offering as an after-school program. To my amazement, he agreed!*

FAMILY DISCUSSION
Allowance

- Sit down with your pre-teen and review what their typical week looks like: when, where and how they are likely to need money and how much is reasonable.

- This is money they are going to spend anyway, so use their allowance to start shifting some of the responsibility to them.

- Making the budgeting process collaborative will give your pre-teen a sense of empowerment and control over their spending. It will also result in buy-in.

Limitations or laissez-faire

Once your child receives his allowance, try to resist the urge to get overly involved in what he does with it. Explain that he should allocate his allowance to the different categories of **SAVE**, **SPEND**, **SHARE** and **INVEST**. You can be somewhat hands-off as his spending should be guided by the budget you created together. Allow him to make his own spending choices and to live with the consequences of his own decisions. However, it's still a good idea to sit down regularly and see if he is managing to stay within budget. The budget may need tweaking if you under- or over-estimated his spending. Also, debriefing about a big purchase or a money mistake is always valuable. We'll discuss this later on in this chapter.

The hardest thing I've had to do as a parent is let my kids fail at something and face the consequences. It's no different with money. They need the freedom to make mistakes and learn from the consequences. I don't rescue them but I also don't say I told you so. I don't always make the right financial decisions either, so it's important for them to see that we all learn from our mistakes.

SAVE

PIGGY BANKS TO REAL BANKS

Around this age, your child is ready to graduate from a piggy bank to a bank account. The advantages of a bank account include the opportunity to earn interest on their savings as well as the security of having their money in a safe place. If you bring your child with you when you open their first account, try to do most of the paperwork with the bank ahead of time. Sometimes these processes take longer than you expect and you don't want your kid to get bored and lose interest — this should be an exciting day!

Some kids may resist because it feels like they are losing their money. So show them their bank balance and how it keeps growing every time they empty their piggy bank (or their savings compartment) to make a deposit. That should encourage them!

"Youth accounts" are special accounts designed for young savers. While generally there are no fees, they also pay very low rates of interest … which makes this the perfect time to discuss the concept of interest with your pre-teen: the bank is paying them to keep their savings there. You may also want to add that if you have to borrow money from the bank, they will *charge* you interest for using their money.

Let your kid know that the bank/debit card they get with their account can be a convenient way to make withdrawals and to check their balance online. (More about debit cards below.) With a youth account, often withdrawals are limited by the bank, for example, up to $20 or $25 per week. Your pre-teen will be responsible for creating and protecting their own PIN, but you may want to reinforce the importance of not telling anyone what their PIN is, not even their close friends.

MATCHING SAVINGS

An effective way to encourage pre-teens to save toward a goal they've chosen is to offer to match their savings. In fact, you may even have experienced matched savings yourself if you work for a company that matches retirement or other savings. Also, if you have contributed to an RESP for your child, the government makes grants of 20% of contributions made to an RESP (up to $500 per beneficiary per year). For the recipient, this is like getting free money, and most rational people would take full advantage!

FAMILY DISCUSSION
ATM use

- Do you think your pre-teen is ready to make unsupervised ATM or bank branch deposits or withdrawals?

- Do you trust them to keep their own bank card and to safeguard their PIN?

CHEQUING ACCOUNTS

While on the topic of bank accounts, you can talk to your pre-teen about how you use a chequing account. Explain that writing a cheque is a way to pay someone that is often more convenient than using cash and also more secure. Only the person to whom the cheque is written can cash it and, unlike cash, if a cheque is lost or stolen you can stop payment on it. Certainly cheques are preferred when you have to mail a payment.

A STORY ABOUT SETTING GOALS

THINGS TO DO
Chequing accounts

- Show your pre-teen how you keep track of the money in your chequing account by recording every cheque you write as well as the other additions to and withdrawals from the account.

- By "balancing" your cheque book (reconciling it to your bank balance), you are modelling financial responsibility for your child.

- You are demonstrating the importance of keeping track of your money, knowing if you have enough to cover any cheques you write or withdrawals you make.

- You can explain that if you "bounce" a cheque, the bank charges a big fee and the recipient doesn't get paid.

- Explain that managing your bank accounts and paying bills online is extremely efficient and convenient.

Emma Taylor and her best friend Allison really wanted iPods. When Allison asked her mom to buy her an iPod, her mom told her to start saving her birthday and Christmas money. She also recommended that Allison save some of her allowance or do some extra work around the house to earn even more money. At first, Allison worked really hard to earn extra income and was really disciplined about putting her savings in her piggy bank. She was well on her way to saving enough for an iPod.

One day when Allison was out with her friends, she told them how much money she had in her piggy bank. Her friends begged her to buy them ice cream. Allison wanted to be generous to her friends so she took some money out of her piggy bank to treat her friends. Next, they wanted to go to the movies and they wanted Allison to pay, since she had so much money. She didn't know how to say no, so she took some more money from her piggy bank. She also sponsored one of her friends in a charity walk. Every day, Allison kept finding more and more interesting things to spend her money on. But she wasn't saving for an iPod any more. When she spent her money on other things, she gave up saving for an iPod.

Emma planned differently. She earned income from doing extra chores around the house. She used her multi-slotted piggy bank to save most of her allowance and birthday money, set a little aside for spending today and some for sharing with others. When Emma's friends begged her to buy them ice cream, candy or movie tickets, she would tell them that she was saving for an iPod. But she would always remember to buy her friends a special treat on their birthday. Before too long,

Emma had saved enough money to buy an iPod.

Emma and Allison met at the mall so Emma could buy her iPod. When they got there, Emma could see that Allison was really upset. Allison had spent all her money and now she couldn't buy the one thing she really wanted—an iPod. Emma felt bad for Allison, but she was also happy that she stuck to her plan and achieved her goal. She not only had enough money for an iPod, she also had a little left over for a pizza, which she shared with Allison to cheer her up.

SPEND

GETTING OUT IN THE WORLD

Today's kids are becoming consumers at an earlier age than kids in the past. By the time they turn 12, they are making a lot of financial decisions on their own. Because our society places a lot of emphasis on consumption, it can be hard for pre-teens to resist the desire to buy things. At this age, they spend money quickly and impulsively. Between the ages of 9 and 12, kids will develop consumption habits that stay with them for the rest of their lives. But they will also learn a lot from the mistakes they make—if you let them.

Spending their own money vs. yours

As we discussed above, giving your kids an allowance is one way to transfer some of the responsibility to them while also helping to reduce requests for money. When kids are spending their own money (even if you give it to them as allowance), they tend to think a lot longer and harder about a potential purchase, whether they really need it or just want it. "It's not worth that much, I don't want it" is something kids say when they have to spend their own money. When they're spending your money, it doesn't seem to "count" in the same way and there is often less deliberation. Decide who pays for what and what comes out of their allowance by referring back to the budget you created together.

My 12-year old brother is much younger than me — 18 years younger — so I often feel like a parent as much as a sister. When I take him to the mall, I remind him to bring his own money, in case he wants to buy something. As we walk through the food court, he always insists he doesn't want anything, he's not hungry — unless someone else offers to pay!

FAMILY DISCUSSION
"Debrief" purchases

When your kids do save up to buy something with their own money, make the time to debrief about it afterwards with the following questions:

- Did they think it was worth the money?

- Was it worth the effort involved in earning it and saving for it?

- What did they enjoy or dislike about the shopping experience?

- What, if anything, would they do differently next time?

Media and advertising

Pre-teens are exposed to a lot of advertising, through the Internet, TV, magazines and product placement. They are also exposed to advertising in public places, like public washrooms, taxis, buses and outdoor billboards. Even though they can distinguish between a programme on TV and a commercial, they don't necessarily understand that the purpose of the commercial is to seduce you into buying things you would not otherwise purchase.

I try to explain to my pre-teen son that commercials are designed to make him think that he <u>needs</u> a certain toy or pair of shoes in order to be happy, when really he just wants them because they're cool. When we watch TV together, I try to get my son to think critically about what he's seeing. I point out how ads exaggerate the benefits of their products and downplay the negative features. We laugh about catch phrases like "healthy-looking skin" (shouldn't it be "healthy skin?"). Better yet, I taught him how to use the PVR to record shows and skip through all the commercials!

Brand names and peer pressure

Even though you still have primary influence over your pre-teen's spending, at this age they rely heavily on what their friends think. By age 12, most kids will side with their peers over their parents when it comes to purchasing decisions. They recognize brands, know which stores they like to shop at, and like to have the latest clothes or electronic devices.

Today's families are smaller than in previous generations, and where there are two people earning salaries, there tends to be more disposable income. Some parents compensate for the lack of quality time spent with their kids by buying them things. This undermines messages about teaching kids the value of a dollar.

Growing up, my family didn't have a lot of disposable income. My parents were able to provide for the necessities, but they could not afford the little extras like the cool brand of shoes or the hottest toy. I want my kids to have more than I had and I want them to fit in. I feel guilty when I say "no" to something they want.

Cell phones

Maybe it's a generational thing, but it's hard for parents today to understand why their kids need a cell phone at such a young age. We have trouble grasping the way kids communicate with each other now—it's so radically different than it was when we were growing up. Every family has to decide for themselves whether a cell phone is appropriate and affordable for their pre-teen.

At this stage, you are most likely to be the one paying the cell phone bill. However, your pre-teen should still be accountable for her usage. Determine how she intends to use the phone and find the most appropriate package. Tell her how many texts or minutes she has per week or month and be very clear about the cost of going over. If she goes over, she should be held accountable to pay the additional costs. Be extra careful about roaming charges. If you travel outside of Canada, you may want to consider asking your kids to leave their phones at home!

FAMILY DISCUSSION
Cell phones

- Is your kid responsible? Will they make sure the phone does not get lost, damaged or stolen?

- Are they self-disciplined? Will they be able to follow rules about usage; for example, not using it in school and turning it off at night?

- Do they need it for safety reasons? Perhaps they walk to school alone or take public transit often. It may make both of you feel better to be reachable.

MORE TEACHABLE MOMENTS

Grocery shopping provides lots of opportunities to teach responsible money management. While you're at home, let your kids help you make the shopping list. Let them see that you plan your meals in advance in order to avoid buying expensive take-out or restaurant meals. Remind them that feeding a family is a significant component of a household budget. Explain that shopping with a list means you are less likely to make impulse purchases and therefore keep within your budget. It also gives you ammunition in the junk food aisle when your kids start pestering you to buy all kinds of stuff: "It's not on our list!"

THINGS TO DO
Comparison shopping

- For fun, do a blind taste test in your house of name brand vs. store brand products to see if you and your kids can tell the difference.

- Try this with soda, cheese, crackers, cookies and paper towels. If your kids do prefer the more expensive brand, ask them if they like it enough to pay the extra money?

Going down the list, your kids can be the runners, picking items off the shelves. You can use this as an opportunity to teach them to comparison shop. Have them compare different brands, including store brands, to see which offer the best value. You can explain to them that the cheapest product doesn't always offer the best value if it isn't good quality. You may also want to point out that name brand products are more expensive than store brand products. This is because the name brand product includes the costs of marketing and advertising.

I like to be thrifty. When my kids were young, they used to help me do the grocery shopping. First we would go through the flyers and the coupons and see what was on sale. At the store, my kids would try to find items in our price range and look for the best value. I remember once asking my son to go get something we needed, but he came back empty-handed: "Mom, it wasn't on sale."

"We can't buy any cereal today, Mommy, it's not on sale!"

49

DEBIT AND CREDIT CARDS

When your pre teen opens a bank account, she will get a bank card that can also be used as a debit card in stores. As with ATM withdrawals, there are usually limits as to how much she can purchase by debit card per day. Make sure your child understands that she must have money in her account to cover debit purchases. Money must first be deposited before it can be spent. Also, it never hurts to remind her to be very careful not to lose her card and not to disclose her PIN to anyone.

Be sure your child understands the difference between a debit card and a credit card. If you haven't done so already, take the time to teach her what a credit card is and how it works (see Chapter 2, p. 33, At the Restaurant). It's also a good idea to discuss the power of compounding, that the amount you owe keeps growing if you do not pay your balance off on the due date (see **Simple vs. Compound Interest** in Chapter 4).

VIRTUAL SPENDING: ITUNES, EBAY, ETC.: HOW DO YOU MAKE THE SPENDING FEEL REAL?

Online spending is relatively new and offers some unique challenges for parents. Just as spending your money does not feel "real" to your pre-teen, making online purchases on iTunes or eBay using their parent's credit card or PayPal account doesn't either. Taking actual cash and handing it over to someone else definitely does! If your kids want to buy music or movies on iTunes, or make other online purchases, consider having them reimburse you in cash.

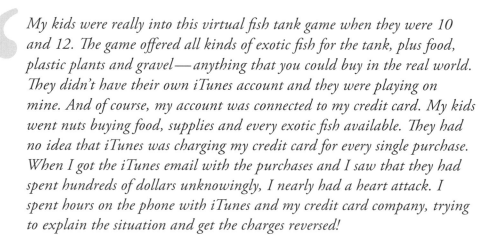

My kids were really into this virtual fish tank game when they were 10 and 12. The game offered all kinds of exotic fish for the tank, plus food, plastic plants and gravel—anything that you could buy in the real world. They didn't have their own iTunes account and they were playing on mine. And of course, my account was connected to my credit card. My kids went nuts buying food, supplies and every exotic fish available. They had no idea that iTunes was charging my credit card for every single purchase. When I got the iTunes email with the purchases and I saw that they had spent hundreds of dollars unknowingly, I nearly had a heart attack. I spent hours on the phone with iTunes and my credit card company, trying to explain the situation and get the charges reversed!

SHARE

FOSTERING AN ATTITUDE OF GRATITUDE

In Chapter 1 we discussed how and why you are important role models for your kids. They don't just absorb your behaviour, but your attitudes too. Fostering an attitude of gratitude begins with you showing appreciation for what you have instead of focusing on what you don't. (If you haven't already done so, take the Role Model Self-Assessment at the end of Chapter 1.) If you don't want your kids to have an attitude of entitlement and take things for granted, then you must continue to show them that you work hard for the money you make, you spend it carefully, you value the things you buy and you look after them.

I think you need to set up expectations for your kids early on. You can't give them everything. They need to earn it. You need to start by being a good role model yourself. I was raised by a single mother, and growing up my mother always kept us in the loop about our family finances. We knew that she could only afford to buy us our favourite toy once a year and we respected that. We treated that toy very well.

Helping those less fortunate

Pre-teens often complain that they're "deprived" because we say "No" to so many of the things they want. One way to put things into perspective for them, as we discussed in Chapter 1, is to show them the household budget, reminding them of all the other needs that have to be provided for. Another way is to help them realize that there are others less fortunate than they are, others they can help. While they may take for granted that they will always have clothes and shoes that fit, there are other children who are not so lucky.

I get my kids to participate in deciding what to do with the toys and books they don't use any more and the clothes that no longer fit. Together we go through their closet and take out any clothes that they can't or don't wear anymore. Then we drop them off at a charity in our community. This teaches them that stuff—even their old stuff—has value and people are grateful to receive it.

INVEST

Although kids this age are too young to understand a lot about investing, here are two ways to introduce them to some basic concepts.

CASHFLOW 101, THE BOARD GAME — MONOPOLY ON STEROIDS!

We tend to focus on teaching kids how to work for money, rather than teaching kids how to make money work for them. After the Taylors had mastered Monopoly, they found a board game called "Cashflow"; the objective of the game is to learn how to make money through investments rather than through pay cheques and to eventually leave the rat race and move to the fast track. Along the way, you acquire real estate, buy start-up companies, pay for children's education and deal with problems like parking tickets and leaky water heaters. By playing Cashflow as a family, the Taylors were able to learn valuable lessons and gain insights into personal finance and investing without having to put their actual money at risk. (There are versions of this game for adults and for kids.)

ENTREPRENEURSHIP REVISITED

Some service businesses, like babysitting or dog walking, do not require much from your pre-teen in the way of "start-up capital". Everything they earn is pure profit. Others, like lawn mowing or snow shovelling may require an upfront investment in equipment. Businesses that involve buying inventory and reselling it, like the proverbial lemonade stand, also require an upfront investment in materials.

FAMILY DISCUSSION
Entrepreneurship

Before your child embarks on her entrepreneurial journey, help her think it through:

- Will I need equipment or materials and how will I pay for them?

- If I need to borrow money for start-up capital, how will I pay it back?

KEY POINTS

- Between the ages of 9 and 12, your kids' understanding of the world is deeper than it was at younger ages. You can help them deepen their understanding of how money works too.

- The money habits that kids form in these years can be the foundation for how they relate to money when they're much older. Help them develop habits that are based on conscious decisions, not impulsive reactions.

- At this stage of their lives, kids are better able to grasp the rationale behind budgeting ... and to become increasingly accountable for how well they stick to their budget.

- As with younger kids, there are plenty of moments in everyday life that lend themselves to conversations about money when your kids are this age. But they're also old enough to benefit from more formal direction—for instance, going to the bank with you to set up their own savings account.

CHAPTER

4

"Thanks, man!"

Teaching Teenagers

GUIDELINES FOR TEENS 13 TO 17 YEARS OLD

The teenage years are a time of transition from carefree childhood to the adult world of responsibilities, including financial responsibilities. Ideally, you have been teaching your kids about money all along, beginning in grade school and progressing as they entered middle school. But what if you haven't — is it too late? No, it's never too late to learn the basics of **EARN**, **SAVE**, **SPEND**, **SHARE** and **INVEST**. But this is a crucial time for your teen to develop sound money management skills. As parents you must lead by example — like it or not, you are financial role models!

It can be difficult to communicate with your teenager about anything at this age, but when it comes to money, try not to make it a taboo subject in your home. Your kids will learn best if you can manage to be open and adopt a positive attitude to discussing money. Be prepared to answer your teen's questions and speak to them as equals. Don't bore them with lectures … and always try to maintain your sense of humour!

> ### FAMILY DISCUSSION
> *Money*
>
> You may want to initiate the conversation about money with some open-ended questions:
>
> - What does money mean to you?
>
> - What does it mean to have a lot of money?
>
> - How much is a lot of money?
>
> - What happens when you cannot pay back what you owe?

EARN

THEIR FIRST "REAL" JOB

Up until now, your kids have earned money by receiving an allowance, from birthday gifts, or as payment for doing odd jobs. Adolescence is usually the time when they get their first "real" job, earning money by working part-time during the year or full-time in the summer. Your teenagers may work in a retail store, selling clothes or scooping ice cream, or even at a fast food restaurant. Unlike the odd jobs they worked in the past, these jobs may require them to have a Social Insurance Number so that they can be paid, and a bank account (if they don't already have one). For the first time they will have a boss, co-workers and shifts — in other words, a lot more responsibility.

You want your teen's first real job to be a positive experience for them. They will need your support as they make the transition from being dependent on you for money to making their own. Motivation is the key to a teenager's initiation to the working world. Encourage them to adopt a positive attitude towards work at a young age—to develop a strong work ethic. You are a role model in this area too, so be aware of your own attitude toward work. Do you wake up energized and excited to get to work or do you experience a sense of dread at the thought of another work week? Whether you realize it or not, they probably know how you really feel about your work.

It can be difficult for teenagers to find jobs because they usually don't have much work experience. They need to be determined and motivated when looking, and they'll need your support in their job search and your guidance in their choice of a job. Most jobs have minimum age requirements of 15 or 16 years. Some teens will be able to handle a part-time job during the school year and still get good grades; for others it may be too much—only you know what's right for your teen.

HELPING THEM UNDERSTAND THEIR PAY CHEQUE

The first pay cheque can be very exciting for your teen! It's worth taking a few minutes to go over the pay stub your teen receives with his cheque, so he understands the difference between "gross" and "net" pay. Explain that employers are required by law to make certain deductions or "withholdings" directly from gross pay (the hourly wage or salary) and send these amounts straight to the government. These may include income tax, Employment Insurance (EI) and Canada Pension Plan (CPP) contribu-

---

THINGS TO DO
Getting a job

Once your teen has decided to get a job, you can help by suggesting the following steps:

1. Apply for a Social Insurance Number (SIN) and card:

   - Go to **www.sdc.gc.ca** and allow six weeks for the card to be processed.

2. Know what you're good at and how to promote yourself:

   - Look for jobs that will allow you to use your strengths and skills.

   - Present yourself with confidence.

3. Seek job interviews:

   - Prepare a resume and cover letter (most teens get help with this in their "Careers" class at school).

   - Walk around your neighbourhood or local mall and ask store owners or managers if they are hiring.

   - Dress appropriately.

   - Act confident and outgoing.

4. Follow up:

   - If you leave your phone number, make sure your voice mail message sounds professional.

   - Follow up with all potential leads.

tions. As a result, your kid's net or "take home" pay may be quite a bit lower than they were expecting.

You may want to explain that in Canada we pay tax at graduated rates, meaning that the tax rate goes up as your income rises. Also we pay income tax to both the federal and provincial governments. There is a tax credit called the Basic Personal Amount ($10,527 for the 2011 tax year). If your teen earns this amount or less in a year, their earnings are not subject to federal tax and generally no tax should be withheld at source.

They may be baffled by CPP and EI. Simply explain that they are programs run by the government, and every person who works must contribute to them. CPP pays benefits to seniors who qualify, and EI protects workers by paying out benefits to those who become unemployed. Make sure they know that their employer also contributes to EI and CPP on their behalf.

Name of Employee: Joe Smith				Name of Employer: ABC Company		
Earning	No. of Hours	Hourly Rate	Amount	Deduction	Amount	Year to Date
Salary	30	9.25	277.50	CPP	12.91	64.55
Overtime Pay	2	13.87	27.74	EI	9.68	48.40
Vacation Pay			17.61	Income Tax	48.43	242.15
Total Earnings			322.85	Total Deductions	71.02	
Pay Period: June 7–June 20, 2011			Pay Date: June 24, 2011		Net Pay: 251.83	

PAYING FOR GOOD GRADES

Some parents find it very difficult to motivate their kids to study. Out of frustration and desperation, they may be tempted to "bribe" their kids to get good grades. But this may give kids the wrong idea — that everything has a price and that they should be paid for every accomplishment. At this early stage, it is better to try to help teens find some intrinsic motivation, some drive within themselves to do their best. Focus on their strengths and the subjects they're good at. Success in these areas becomes self-reinforcing. You can also remind them that learning good study habits, like learning good money habits, will serve them well as they progress through school and hopefully on to higher learning.

In our family, my parents rewarded us with "bonuses" when we made the honour role at school. But rather than give us the money, they put our bonus into an RESP to encourage and motivate us to go to university.

ONLINE CONSIGNMENT SALES

Do people still hold garage sales? It seems like anyone with anything to sell these days does it online using eBay, Craigslist or social media sites. Looking around your house, you probably have lots of items that are perfectly good but are no longer useful to your family. Consider having your teen sell some of those items online. Remember the Three Cs we introduced in Chapter 1 — create, conserve, convert? Well, this is a great example of convert. Think of it as a consignment sale. They are selling items on your behalf and as a result are entitled to keep a portion of the proceeds of sale. Whether you split the proceeds 50/50 or some other way is entirely up to you and your teen — and it will be a good test of their negotiating skills! It's a win-win proposition — the more they are able to get for the item, the more you both make.

"Thanks, man!"

My son is 16 and has been playing guitar since he was nine. We bought him his first electric guitar as a birthday gift and for a long time it was suitable for his skill level. But as he progressed, he really wanted a better guitar. He did some research to figure out what he wanted to buy and what it would cost. Then we sat down to figure out how we were going to pay for it. My son came up with his own version of the Three Cs: he would <u>create</u> wealth by doing extra chores, he would <u>conserve</u> his allowance by spending less on snacks after school, and he would <u>convert</u> his old guitar into cash by selling it on Craigslist!

SAVE

CASH IS KING

Try introducing your teen to the expression *"Cash is king"*. It applies equally to businesses and to individuals. When you have cash or other financial resources, you are in command, you call the shots. You have the resources to ride out difficult times, and you also have the capital to take advantage of opportunities that arise. On the other hand, being in debt is like being enslaved. The interest on the debt you carry and the debt itself is like an albatross around your neck. (As we discussed in Chapter 1, not all debt is bad. There is such a thing as good debt — debt incurred for the purpose of acquiring an asset that has the potential to go up in value, such as your house.)

The best place for your teen to save money is in the bank. Almost every teenager should have his or her own bank account. If your child expresses interest (pun intended), you can make sure they understand that the way a bank makes money is by earning a "spread". The interest rate they pay you on your savings is lower than the interest rate they charge on amounts that their customers borrow.

Help your teen to determine what type of account is best for them (chequing or savings). Investigate whether they still qualify for a youth account, as most fees are waived. At this stage, you can assume that your teen will be accessing the ATM machine on her own. Remind her that ATMs found in restaurants and most convenience stores charge very high fees. A $20 withdrawal may end up costing her $2.50 to $4.00 in fees. Encourage her to plan her cash needs ahead of time and use an ATM owned by her bank, where withdrawals are free.

Of course, teenagers can't apply for credit cards until they reach the age of majority, which is either 18 or 19, depending on their province of residence. However, they can benefit from learning about the responsible use of credit cards. We will revisit this topic in Chapter 5.

USING PERSONAL VALUES TO SET SMART GOALS

In Chapter 1, we introduced the idea of using your values to set meaningful goals. Values are the things in life that are most important to you, that you are willing to take a stand for. You can get a sense of what people value by the way they dress, how they spend their money or how they interact with others. Values are intangible, but they are not invisible to others. You may think your kids will absorb your values about money by osmosis, be they power, friendship, connection, adventure, fun or security. But as we suggested in Chapter 1, kids are exposed to a lot of conflicting messages about money, so it's important to be clear and explicit about your family values and how they impact your financial decisions.

If they haven't done it already, get your kids to try the Values Validator at the end of Chapter 1. Their values will help them prioritize their spending and set SMART savings goals.

FAMILY DISCUSSION
Goal setting

Discuss SMART goals with your kids. They are:

- Specific
- Measurable
- Attainable and Action-oriented
- Realistic
- Time-framed

When Emma Taylor completed the Values Validator, she determined that her top five values were: adventure, friendship, health, academics and security. She focused on adventure, doing new and interesting things, and developed a very meaningful SMART goal for herself. Here is Emma's Goal-Setting Worksheet.

EMMA TAYLOR'S GOAL-SETTING WORKSHEET*

TOP 5 VALUES	TOP 5 FINANCIAL GOALS	MAKE SPECIFIC, MEASURABLE, ATTAINABLE and ACTION-ORIENTED	48-HOUR PLAN What actions will you take in the next 48 hours?	ENLIST HELP Who will you share your goals with?	TIME-FRAME When will you finish?
Example: Adventure	Save up for a trip to Europe after high school graduation.	$3,000 will be needed by July 1, 2013	Go online and research the cost of the trip. Calculate how much I can make if I work full-time over the next two summers and part-time during the school year.	Speak to my manager at work about adding shifts. Discuss the travel budget with my parents and get their feedback.	In 2 years, I will need to book the airfare and have enough money saved for hotels, trains, food and shopping.
Friendship					
Health					
Academics					
Security					

* Adapted from The Purpose-Focused Financial Plan worksheet *in The Finish Rich Workbook*, David Bach (*Toronto: Doubleday Canada, 2005*).

For another example of a goal-setting worksheet, please see the end of this chapter.

PAYING THEMSELVES FIRST
— AND MAKING IT AUTOMATIC

Living within your means is arguably the most important lesson you can teach your kids. And the best way to teach it is to put your money where your mouth is: do not spend more than you make. Easier said than done, right? Wrong! You can make sure you don't spend more than you make by paying yourself first. And this is exactly what your teenager should be doing with the money he makes too.

Every month, he should take a certain amount of money directly from his earnings and put it into savings. A rule of thumb is to save 10% of what you earn. If that seems like too much at first, then begin with 5%. If 10% is easily achieved, then increase it to 15% or 20%. To make sure it happens, have him set it up as an automatic transfer. Save him from himself—he will able to spend only what remains. Having a SMART goal that he's saving for, one that ties back to his values, will make saving meaningful and rewarding and will increase his chances of success.

SPEND

Once your kids hit the teen years, they tend to want to spend all their time with their friends. Teenage girls especially enjoy going shopping and hanging out at the mall. Sometimes it even feels like they go out of their way to avoid you! You don't have as many teachable moments as you did when they were younger, when they would accompany you to the grocery store or the mall. They are much more interested in the opinions of their friends when it comes to consuming, but they are also better able to assert their individuality than they were just a few years earlier. However, as long as they are still living under your roof, you can find the right time to instill good spending habits.

ALLOWANCE: INCREASED FINANCIAL RESPONSIBILITY

Whether your teen is working or not, they still need an allowance. But use it to begin gradually transferring more financial responsibilities to them. They can use the allowance to cover their basic needs and some of their wants. As we will discuss under **Budgeting**, the budget should be the basis for determining their allowance, which should be given to your teen regularly—weekly, bi-weekly, or monthly.

If your teen is also working, should they be allowed to spend the money they earn however they want? Teens want to be independent, and you should let them make their own money choices and live with the consequences. But first give them some guidance and support or they are liable to make some unwise decisions.

BUDGETING

Teens don't have much overhead if they live at home because you're still taking care of most of their needs. As a result, they don't know what their lives really cost. A mistake teenagers often make, especially if they don't have savings goals, is to use all their income on "discretionary" spending.

There is no shortage of items tempting your teen to spend their money: video games, electronics, clothes, shoes, junk food, etc. These temptations can be difficult to resist at any age. While kids can technically get away with blowing their money at this age, it establishes a bad habit that may be hard to break once they get older and they do have to worry about rent, food, transportation and utilities — all the mundane essentials.

As we mentioned in Chapter 3, it's a good idea to regularly review the budget with your teen to see if it needs fine-tuning. The review process also ensures that she feels accountable for staying within budget, and can provide an explanation as to why she was under- or over-budget. Just like in the "real world", things will come up from time to time and your teen may decide she wants to "rob from Peter to pay Paul". In other words, she wants to redirect funds from one budget category to another. That's fine — all budgets are flexible — as long as she does it intentionally and can account for it. For a sample teen budget, see the Teen Budget template at the end of this chapter.

THINGS TO DO
Budget

- Work with your teen to create a budget (If your kid has been budgeting from a younger age, all the better!)

- Calculate a reasonable amount for transportation and clothing, being careful to hold your ground on needs vs. wants.

- Work out an entertainment budget by figuring out how many movies or dinners are reasonable per month.

- Have your kid save receipts so she can keep track of what she spends and you can review the details.

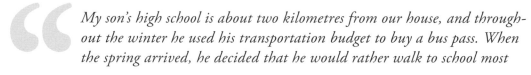

My son's high school is about two kilometres from our house, and throughout the winter he used his transportation budget to buy a bus pass. When the spring arrived, he decided that he would rather walk to school most

days and put the money towards other things, such as records for his vinyl collection. Together we decided that he would buy 10 bus tickets, so he always had some on hand for getting around on the weekend or after school, and that he could use the rest of the money at his own discretion.

Especially with teens, it is important to let them make mistakes and learn their lessons. Although the stakes are higher than they were at a younger age, we're still not talking about thousand-dollar mistakes. Letting them "waste" their money on something they don't need, or that's of low quality, can teach them a lot about value … but only if you take the time to discuss it.

"

My 16-year-old daughter went through a "Starbucks phase" where she was stopping often on her way home from school and buying fancy expensive coffees. She didn't realize how these little purchases were adding up. When the weekend rolled around, she made plans with her friends to see a movie. But as she got ready to go, she checked her wallet and realized she had spent most of her money and didn't have enough to see a movie. She wanted me to give her the shortfall but I wouldn't. I wanted her to learn that when you make choices about how to spend your money, you have to live with the consequences—even if it meant "ruining her social life."

TRACKING SPENDING

In Chapter 1, we explained why it's so important for you to track spending: it makes you more aware of your spending habits. It's a great reality check for your kid too. They often think they're spending according to the plan — until they face the figures on the page and see that their tracking shows a very different spending pattern! And as with all of us, seeing it in writing can motivate them to make better spending choices going forward.

The Taylors used the "jar system" to teach Emma to track her spending. She no longer had a piggy bank, of course, but she had three jars in her room, labelled "clothing", "entertainment" and "transportation". Emma would allocate her budget to each of the three categories. As she spent money from the jar, she would replace the money spent with a receipt. She could see quite easily how much money was left in her budget in each category at any time. When she got to the end of the money in a jar, she could no longer spend in that category, unless she chose to take it from a different category.

Although the Taylors used a very low-tech system with Emma, there are lots of different "money apps" for smartphones that allow you to track your spending in real time. These apps may appeal to teens who are already using their phones to do just about everything else.

NEEDS VS. WANTS AGAIN

Just like younger kids, teens need to be reminded of the difference between needs and wants. Remind them to ask themselves that all-important question: do I need it or would it just be nice to have it? Help them understand that they have to take their resources (time and money) into account when making purchasing decisions.

> **FAMILY DISCUSSION**
> *Needs vs. Wants*
>
> Help your teen assess the relative cost of a want by asking them:
>
> - How many hours would you have to work to be able to buy it?
> - Does that feel reasonable?
> - What are you giving up by spending your money in that way?

It can be shocking to see how sophisticated some teens' tastes are and to watch them covet certain brands. This can be an opportunity to talk to them about marketing and branding. Show them that companies spend a lot of money advertising their products to convince you that you "need" them. Teens are subject to as much, if not more, advertising than younger kids. As parents, you can help your teen think critically and sceptically about the messages they get through advertising.

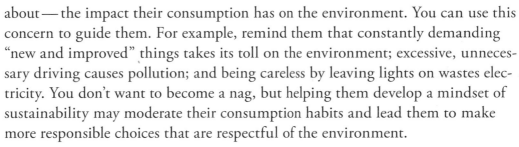

> *I get really excited if I'm about to buy something new, but after I buy it, it never makes me as happy as I think it's going to.*

AN ECOLOGICAL APPROACH TO FINANCIAL RESPONSIBILITY

Compared to younger kids, teenagers seem to be more aware of—and more concerned about—the impact their consumption has on the environment. You can use this concern to guide them. For example, remind them that constantly demanding "new and improved" things takes its toll on the environment; excessive, unnecessary driving causes pollution; and being careless by leaving lights on wastes electricity. You don't want to become a nag, but helping them develop a mindset of sustainability may moderate their consumption habits and lead them to make more responsible choices that are respectful of the environment.

SPENDING WISELY

Even though teens (hopefully!) have more maturity and self-discipline than younger kids, their brains are still developing and they still often tend to act on impulse ... but you can help. Encourage your teen to shop around and compare prices as a way to stretch their budget and get more for their hard-earned money. Help them look for coupons, sales or promotions. Let them see how much they can save by taking a patient and disciplined approach to shopping.

> *Money was tight in my family when I was growing up. At Christmas time, my mom used to give my siblings and me each $10. She told us to use the $10 to buy a Christmas gift for each member of the family. $10 is not a lot of money so you really had to shop wisely to stretch your budget. This was a very good skill to learn.*

STORED VALUE CARDS

Because they can be difficult to shop for, teens tend to get gift cards as presents. Teach them to read the fine print: some gift cards have expiry dates. Also, the cards tend to get forgotten in the back of their wallets unless kids are proactive about using them. Get them to make a list of all the gift cards they have and their remaining balances and to make a plan to spend them before they expire. And remind them that the cards are usually not replaceable, so they should be sure to keep them in a place where they will not lose them.

NEGOTIATING AND BARGAINING

In some places in the world, negotiating and bargaining when making purchases is the norm — in fact, it's expected. Not so in Canada. In most retail stores, especially large chains, the price as displayed is the price you pay at the cash, unless it's on sale. However, at smaller boutiques, you may be able to get a discount if you ask. It always pays to ask whether the price displayed is actually the best price available.

And don't forget to tell your teen to budget for sales tax when buying something. Some may not realize that taxes are not normally included in the prices of goods but are additional costs. In some provinces, the total sales tax can be as high as 15%.

TIPPING

Next time you are out for dinner with your teen, talk to them about tipping. They may already know about it, but if they don't, it's pretty certain they'll need to know before too long — they'll soon be going out to eat on their own with friends. They may not know that servers rely on tips because their hourly wage is very low. You can teach them that the tip is calculated on the total *before* tax and is usually 15–20% for good to excellent service.

SHARE

RAISING MONEY *AT* SCHOOL

Wander the halls of your teenager's school and you will see flyers announcing Terry Fox runs, Me to We events, United Way bake sales — you name it! Schools encourage their student bodies to get involved in fundraising and donating money to causes that they are passionate about. The school wants to foster a sense of community and the satisfaction involved when you give back and many students spend time volunteering for community service projects as well.

If your teen connects with one of the fundraising projects going on at school, encourage him to get involved. But if nothing resonates with him, then perhaps he could establish a new fundraising initiative at the school by speaking to a teacher or the Vice Principal.

One of the most successful and popular fundraising events at my school was Faculty Follies. We approached three well-known and well-liked teachers at our school and we asked them to participate. Their role was to commit to do something outrageous, like grow a moustache and dye it pink, dress up as a Star Wars character, or shave their head. Then we set up three large jars and asked students to contribute spare change towards the outrageous act that they most wanted to see. There were no costs involved so we were able to donate 100% of the proceeds to charity. The "winning" teacher had to dress up like Darth Vader and teach all of his classes in a Star Wars costume!

RAISING MONEY *FOR* SCHOOL

Sometimes, the beneficiary of the school's fundraising efforts is the school itself. Schools have budgets too and there never seems to be enough money to go around. Our public schools are funded by the government, but the cutbacks in recent years have left the schools scrambling to make ends meet. Rather than make further cuts to programs, schools often establish foundations and have fundraising campaigns.

"
*Last fall, my son's high school had an
unusual fundraiser. Rather than the typical
funfair, they held an event called 24-Hour
Relay. Each student had to raise at least
$25 for the chance to spend 24 hours
camping out on the back field of the school!
The field was divided into "girls' camp"
and "boys' camp". They brought portable
camping stoves so they could cook their
meals and they slept in tents. (Our son
begged us to deliver a pizza to his tent!)
The event was sanctioned by the school and
supervised by school staff. It was definitely
one of the highlights of his school year!*

INVEST

INVESTING FOR SHORT- AND MEDIUM-TERM GOALS

Most teenagers don't have a lot of money to invest. Whatever money they're not
spending on immediate purchases, they are probably just stashing in a savings
account to spend at a later date. But as they start to develop longer-term goals, they
need to understand the relationship between goals and investments as well as some
investing basics. Help them understand that their goal or investment objective, the
length of time they have to reach their goals (investment time horizon), and their
appetite for taking risks (risk tolerance) will determine what type of investment is
appropriate in the circumstances. We will cover this in more detail in Chapter 5.

A short-term goal means you will need the money in a few weeks or a few months
(say to buy a gift) and a bank account is generally the most appropriate savings
vehicle. You will earn a low rate of interest but the funds are 100% safe and liquid,
meaning easily cashable. Short of the bank collapsing, you will always be able to
get your money when you need it.

With a medium-term goal, say one to five years, you have more investment options.
You can purchase a term deposit or Guaranteed Investment Certificate (GIC) at

the bank with a term that matches your goal. The longer the term, the longer the money is locked in and the more interest you will earn; also, the interest rate on term deposits and GICs is higher than the interest rate on a savings account. The interest earned will encourage your child to save as it helps them reach their goal faster. The fact that a GIC cannot normally be cashed in before it matures reinforces the concept of delayed gratification.

Say your 15-year-old son has saved a substantial amount over the years (from birthday money, holiday gifts, baby-sitting, odd jobs, etc.) and is saving for a car that he plans to buy before he goes to university in three years. He could purchase a three-year term deposit or GIC with a fixed rate of interest, compounded annually. He will know exactly what he will earn, assuming he holds the GIC until maturity. Again, the principal is guaranteed so there is no way he can lose his investment. But the funds are frozen for this three-year period, and penalties apply if the investment is cashed before the maturity date.

A longer-term goal requires different planning. You can choose investments with growth potential. Because you have a much longer time horizon, you can take advantage of time and let compounding work for you. With these criteria, you have many more investment options available, which we will cover in Chapter 5.

I taught my teenager about the "Rule of 72". It's a simple formula that tells you how long it will take to double your money with compound interest. Divide the number 72 by the interest rate you earn each year. For example, if you have $1,000 invested at 6% compounded annually, divide 72 by 6 to get 12. You will double your money in 12 years.

SIMPLE VS. COMPOUND INTEREST

Simple interest is when the bank pays you a stated rate of interest for a stated period of time on your original deposit, which is called the "principal". Let's say the bank is offering a savings account at 3% simple interest and you deposit $100. Once a year, the bank will pay you 3% of $100, or $3, and add it to the balance in your savings account. After one year, your balance would be $103. At the end of the second year, you would earn an additional $3 of interest and your balance would be $106. After 10 years, you would have earned $30 of interest and have a balance of $130. After 20 years you would have $160.

Compound interest is when you earn interest on your interest. The "magic" of compound interest is that it allows your savings to grow much more quickly. Let's say the bank is offering a savings account at 3% interest "compounded annually". This means that the interest you earn each year is added to your principal and becomes the new basis for calculating the following year's interest. As in the example above, you receive $3 in the first year, so at the end of the year you have $103. But here's the difference: at the end of the second year, interest is calculated at 3% of $103, so you now earn $3.09, giving you a balance of $106.09. After 10 years, you would have earned $34.39 and would have a balance of $134.39 versus $130 with simple interest. After 20 years you would have $180.61 — that's $20.61 more than you would earn with simple interest.

When you are earning a higher interest rate and have a longer period of time to invest, compounding can make a huge difference. That's why it's so important for kids to develop good saving habits early — to take full advantage of the power of compounding and let their money work for them, rather than the other way around.

	SIMPLE INTEREST			COMPOUND INTEREST			
	PRINCIPAL	PRINCIPAL		PRINCIPAL		PRINCIPAL	
	Beginning of Year	Interest	End of Year	Beginning of Year	Interest	End of Year	Difference
Year 1	$100.00	$3.00	$103.00	$100.00	$3.00	$103.00	$—
Year 2	100.00	3.00	106.00	103.00	3.09	106.09	$0.09
Year 3	100.00	3.00	109.00	106.09	3.18	109.27	$0.27
Year 4	100.00	3.00	112.00	109.27	3.28	112.55	$0.55
Year 5	100.00	3.00	115.00	112.55	3.38	115.93	$0.93
Year 6	100.00	3.00	118.00	115.93	3.48	119.41	$1.41
Year 7	100.00	3.00	121.00	119.41	3.58	122.99	$1.99
Year 8	100.00	3.00	124.00	122.99	3.69	126.68	$2.68
Year 9	100.00	3.00	127.00	126.68	3.80	130.48	$3.48
Year 10	100.00	3.00	130.00	130.48	3.91	134.39	$4.39

	SIMPLE INTEREST			COMPOUND INTEREST			
	PRINCIPAL	PRINCIPAL		PRINCIPAL		PRINCIPAL	
	Beginning of Year	Interest	End of Year	Beginning of Year	Interest	End of Year	Difference
Year 11	100.00	3.00	133.00	134.39	4.03	138.42	$5.42
Year 12	100.00	3.00	136.00	138.42	4.15	142.58	$6.58
Year 13	100.00	3.00	139.00	142.58	4.28	146.85	$7.85
Year 14	100.00	3.00	142.00	146.85	4.41	151.26	$9.26
Year 15	100.00	3.00	145.00	151.26	4.54	155.80	$10.80
Year 16	100.00	3.00	148.00	155.80	4.67	160.47	$12.47
Year 17	100.00	3.00	151.00	160.47	4.81	165.28	$14.28
Year 18	100.00	3.00	154.00	165.28	4.96	170.24	$16.24
Year 19	100.00	3.00	157.00	170.24	5.11	175.35	$18.35
Year 20	100.00	3.00	160.00	175.35	5.26	180.61	$20.61

This is also a good time to explain that compound interest is a double-edged sword. It's great when you're a saver and it's working for you. But if you're a borrower, it works just as hard against you. Interest on debt compounds quickly and becomes quite burdensome, especially when interest rates are very high, as they are on credit card balances.

KEY POINTS

- Your kid's first "real" job presents a great opportunity to introduce them to the working world—going over their first pay stub with them, explaining about income tax, CPP and EI teaches a lot about how our society works.

- Teens are not too young to set meaningful financial goals; the clearer their goals, the more likely they are to achieve them.

- School-sponsored programs can be a good opportunity for kids to learn about giving back. Sometimes they can even initiate a charitable program and get the school to endorse it.

- Some teens may be interested in learning some of the basic concepts of investing; the sooner they learn them, the better prepared they'll be when they actually have money to invest.

Resources

TEEN BUDGET TEMPLATE

Category	Monthly Budget	Actual Amount	Difference
	Monthly Budget for Teens		
INCOME:	Estimate Your Income	Your Actual Income	
Wages/Income Pay cheque, allowance, Birthday money, etc.			
Interest Income From savings account			
INCOME SUBTOTAL			
EXPENSES:	Estimate your Expenses	Your Actual Expenses	
Savings Savings account			
Bills Taxes—from pay cheque			
Food/snacks			
Transportation			
Clothing			
Other shopping			
Entertainment e.g., movies, restaurants, video games, music			
EXPENSES SUBTOTAL			
NET INCOME			

Resources

GOAL-SETTING WORKSHEET[1]

TOP 5 VALUES	TOP 5 FINANCIAL GOALS	MAKE SPECIFIC, MEASURABLE, ATTAINABLE and ACTION-ORIENTED	48-HOUR PLAN What actions will you take in the next 48 hours?	ENLIST HELP Who will you share your goals with?	TIME-FRAME When will you finish?
Example: 1. Security	Increase net worth by 10% next year	Increase contributions to RRSP by $200 per pay cheque.	Call benefits person at work; change contributions plan by Friday	Call Pete (financial advisor) to review investment options in RRSP	In 2 weeks, the new investment plan will begin
2. Family					
3. Health					
4. Self-realization/self-development					
5. Community					

1 Adapted from the Purpose-Focused Financial Plan worksheet in *The Finish Rich Workbook*, David Bach (Toronto: Doubleday Canada, 2005).

CHAPTER

5

"It's like totally delicious—wait till you try it. And it _only_ costs $5.95."

Teaching Emerging Adults

GUIDELINES FOR YOUNG ADULTS 18 TO 21 YEARS OLD

Your son or your daughter will always be your child, but at this stage, they hardly seem like children any longer! He or she has finished high school and has emerged from adolescence into young adulthood. They have now reached the age of majority, which means they can legally take on more responsibilities: voting, entering into contracts, serving on a jury or even marrying! They may also be considering going on to college or university.

Post-secondary study is a good example of the concept of "opportunity cost" — the most valuable alternative you give up by choosing another, mutually exclusive option. Some kids at this age may be tempted to start working full-time and earning money rather than going on to do further studying. But, while students who go on to university or college give up the opportunity to earn income right away, they know that they will more than make up for it with higher earning potential after they graduate. Arguably, a university education more than pays for itself over time, and the opportunity costs in this case are minimal. In other situations, the opportunity costs may be significant. Say your child is considering two very different career paths, banker or social worker. The opportunity cost of choosing a career as a social worker rather than a banker is quite high in terms of fore-gone earnings. It may still be the right choice for your son or daughter, based on many other considerations, but encourage them to think carefully about alternatives and to consider the opportunity costs when making decisions.

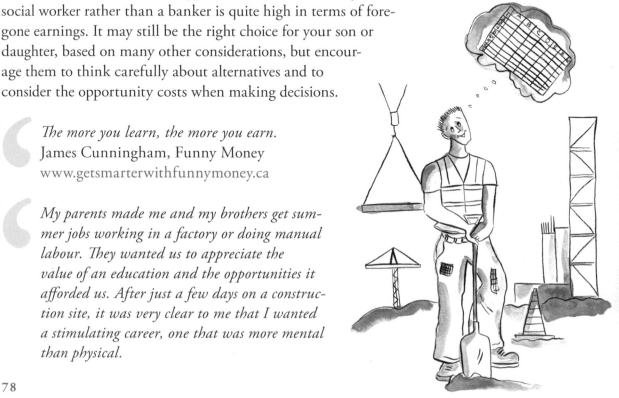

> *The more you learn, the more you earn.*
> James Cunningham, Funny Money
> www.getsmarterwithfunnymoney.ca

> *My parents made me and my brothers get summer jobs working in a factory or doing manual labour. They wanted us to appreciate the value of an education and the opportunities it afforded us. After just a few days on a construction site, it was very clear to me that I wanted a stimulating career, one that was more mental than physical.*

EARN

Your kid may be one of the fortunate ones, that is, they may know they can count on you to pay for their university education—which allows them the luxury of not working and gives them more time to focus on their studies during the school year. Or maybe your kid will be working part-time during the school year or full-time during the summer to help pay for university. If your kid did not work as a teenager, you may want to go back to Chapter 4 and read the sections entitled **Their First "Real" Job** and **Helping Them Understand their Pay Cheque**. This is also a good time to talk to them about the responsibility of filing a tax return.

Throughout high school, Emma Taylor worked part-time at the Gap with her friend Allison. After graduation, Emma went to university out of town. Allison's family couldn't afford to send her away to school, so she lived at home and went to university. She also needed to keep working to help pay her tuition. Allison debated the pros and cons of keeping her job at the Gap. On the one hand, she had a track record of good performance and she had a little seniority, plus she wouldn't have to embark on a job search. On the other hand, as Emma pointed out, she might be limiting herself if she stayed. Prospective employers want people who have had experience from a variety of jobs in different fields. Allison agreed that different work experience would be good—she knew she didn't want to work at her Gap job forever—so she decided to look for a more challenging, better paying job in her area of interest, using the tips outlined in Chapter 4. She ended up finding a position at the university, which employs a lot of students in different administrative and teaching-related positions.

THINGS TO DO
Taxes

Reasons to file a Tax Return:

- To recover any overpaid tax or other source deductions (e.g., CPP, EI) that your employer may have withheld from your pay cheque and remitted to the government.

- To create contribution room in a Registered Retirement Savings Plan (RRSP).

WHY FILE A TAX RETURN?

Some kids may not see the point of filing a tax return, especially if they haven't made very much money. If you are a resident of Canada for all or part of a tax year, you must file a tax return if you either owe tax or you think you may be entitled to a refund. Generally, you must file your return and pay your taxes by April 30th of the year following the tax year. As we discussed in Chapter 4, if your kid's taxable income falls under the Basic Personal Amount (of $10,527 in 2011), then it is unlikely that they will owe tax.

We will discuss RRSPs and TFSAs in the next section.

TAX BREAKS FOR STUDENTS

Students are entitled to deduct some of the costs associated with their post-secondary studies. These deductions take the form of special tax credits that can be used to reduce any income taxes they owe.

There are rules that set out how much can be claimed and (of course!) forms have to be completed. You can learn more by visiting the Canada Revenue Agency's website (**www.cra-arc.gc.ca/tx/ndvdls/tpcs/ncm-tx/rtrn/ cmpltng/ddctns/lns300-350/323/menu-eng.html**).

> **THINGS TO DO**
> *Tax credits*
>
> Claim tax credits for:
> * Tuition fees
> * Education amount
> * Textbook amount

Your child must claim these amounts first, even if you are the one paying. But if your child doesn't need these credits to reduce his or her income (e.g., because it is already below the Basic Personal Amount), then they can be transferred to your return to reduce your taxes (or to a grandparent). They can also be carried forward indefinitely and claimed in any future year.

If your child is moving to attend full-time post-secondary studies, they may be able to claim their moving expenses if:
* they receive scholarships and bursaries while at school that are included in their income
* they move at least 40 kilometres closer to attend school.

Students often take public transit and there is a tax credit available for anyone (not just students) who purchases a public transit pass. It is called the Public Transit Amount and covers *monthly* or *annual passes* (not individual tickets) for unlimited travel within Canada on local buses, streetcars, subways, commuter trains or buses, and local ferries. Remind your child to keep receipts or expired passes as proof of this claim.

SCHOLARSHIPS AND BURSARIES

If your child receives a scholarship, fellowship or bursary, the income will not be subject to tax if they qualify to claim an "education amount" on their tax return.

They have to be enrolled in a "qualifying educational program" at a "designated educational institution" and must be enrolled full-time (or part time due to a disability or mental or physical impairment). Qualifying programs must run for at least three consecutive weeks and include at least ten hours of instruction or work per week. Generally, Canadian universities, colleges and other post-secondary institutions qualify, as do universities outside Canada under certain circumstances.

SAVE

Some young adults decide to work full-time after high school, which means they are in a position to begin a savings program or contribute more to a savings program which they started earlier. On the other hand, if your child is attending university or college, these are likely to be spending, not saving, years. She may have some short-term savings goals from time to time, but if she is earning any money, most of it is probably being spent on university tuition, books and living costs. Your kid probably has a savings and/or a chequing account for managing day-to-day spending and, if you haven't done so already, review the basic mechanics of managing a bank account that we covered in Chapters 3 and 4. It is also worth the time to investigate whether your bank offers a special account for post-secondary students. If they do, your child may be entitled to services at discounted prices. Because you have already introduced your kid to the topic of income tax, take this opportunity to discuss using tax-advantaged savings vehicles as a way to minimize taxes.

TAX-ADVANTAGED SAVINGS

Tax-Free Savings Account (TFSA)

A TFSA is a special savings vehicle for Canadians 18 or older. The annual contribution limit is $5,000 (indexed for inflation). Contributions to the account are *not* tax-deductible — they come out of after-tax earnings. However, income earned inside the account is not subject to tax, nor are amounts withdrawn. If you withdraw an amount from your account, you can re-contribute that amount in the following year, in addition to that year's $5,000 limit. If you don't have the funds to contribute, you can carry forward that amount indefinitely.

For these reasons, a TFSA is a very flexible tool for saving. It can be used to save for a down payment on a house or for an emergency fund, for example. Once you decide what you are saving for, you can choose the appropriate investments to hold and any income is earned tax-free, allowing your savings to grow more quickly. We will discuss investing later in this chapter.

Registered Retirement Savings Plan (RRSP)

If your kid's income doesn't all have to go toward college or university expenses, starting an RRSP can be a good idea. Make sure they know the basics of how RRSPs work. An RRSP is a savings vehicle created by the government to help Canadians save for retirement. Unlike a TFSA, amounts contributed to an RRSP *are* tax-deductible—they come out of pre-tax income, not after-tax earnings. The funds inside an RRSP are invested and the investment income earned inside an RRSP is not subject to tax. This means the investments can grow more quickly to help you reach your long-term goals. And remember, the power of compounding means that even a little bit saved early and often can make a big difference over time.

You must have "earned income" in order to contribute to an RRSP. There are rules about how much you can contribute each year and you must file a tax return. The funds are not taxed until withdrawn at retirement, unless you decide to take the funds out early. There is a special exception for withdrawals made to purchase or build a "qualifying home". In that scenario, you may withdraw up to $25,000 tax-free from your RRSP but you must repay the money to your RRSP within 15 years.

THE "LATTE FACTOR®"[1]

Saving money is challenging for most people, especially for students who may feel like they are living a bare-bones existence in order to make ends meet. If your kids (or you) are looking to save a few dollars every week, you may want to examine your

"It's like totally delicious—wait till you try it. And it *only* costs $5.95."

---

1   www.finishrich.com/lattefactor/

"latte factor". Everybody has one—it's those little indulgences that you could either cut back on or eliminate altogether. Examples are fancy coffees, bottled water, fast food or magazines. Giving up unhealthy and expensive habits like smoking is another great example. We often don't even realize how much we're actually spending on these little purchases, but they add up! Changing your habits may mean more money to pay for tuition and other costs of living.

SPEND

When your child decides to go to university, they are taking the first big step toward independence, a career and financial security. It can be quite a challenging time, especially if they'll be living away from home in a different town or city for the first time. And because the cost of a university education is substantial, financial planning will be required.

PAYING FOR POST-SECONDARY EDUCATION

There are different ways to finance a university education and they are not mutually exclusive. Depending on your circumstances, you may find yourself using some combination of: your savings, which may take the form of withdrawals from an RESP, your current earnings/cash flow, scholarships your child may receive, your child's savings, or their own earnings.

Finally, there are loans—either student loans, or amounts borrowed from a personal line of credit or from other sources. This kind of debt is an example of "good debt"; a university education is an investment in your child's future career and earning power. However, they still need a plan to pay off that debt within a reasonable period of time. Carrying that much debt may delay or alter other goals, such as travelling, buying a house or getting married. The Federal Task Force on Financial Literacy has recommended that the government integrate a financial literacy component into the Canada Student Loans Program for students receiving funding. This may take the form of mandatory counselling about credit and debt.

If your child does get student loans under the *Canada Student Loans Act*, the *Canada Students Financial Assistance Act* or similar provincial or territorial government laws, then they can claim most of the interest paid as a tax credit. If they do not use the credit, they can carry it forward for five years. The tax credit cannot be transferred to anyone else, even if someone else paid the interest on the loan. Also, they cannot claim interest paid on any other kind of loan, such as a personal loan or line of credit.

Perhaps an ideal solution to the issue of paying for university is a co-op program, which also gives participants valuable work experience. Many universities offer these programs and help arrange the placements, which are usually for one semester. Students are paid for their work during that period and return to school at the end of the placement. Although working in a co-op program may mean it will take longer for the student to graduate (since students do not normally get credits for their work terms), the additional income is necessary for many kids to complete their education. And the practical experience can be invaluable: these placements often lead to permanent job offers if the student performs well. Even in the absence of a job offer, co-op placements give the student an opportunity for some "real world" experience in his chosen field and can help him make a more informed career choice.

IS YOUR KID PREPARED TO BE ON HER OWN?

In Chapter 4 we introduced budgeting for teens, getting them used to the responsibility of managing their money, even though you were still taking care of most of their needs. Once they emerge into adulthood, whether into the workforce or to university, they will need to be even more in control of their financial situation. They will need to know what is coming in and what is going out as they try to balance the inflows and outflows.

Your child should get into the habit of tracking his spending—it's really the only way to bring awareness to where the money is going. The accountability that comes with careful tracking can lead to making better spending choices. It will also let him compare his actual spending to his budget, to see where he is on track or where he may be over- or

FAMILY DISCUSSION
Budget

- Encourage your child to create a realistic budget—based on either weekly, bi-weekly or monthly amounts—using the Post-Secondary Student Budget at the end of this chapter.

- Remind them that it's better to be conservative in their planning than to run out of money:

  — Caution them not to overstate income.

  — Remind them to be specific and realistic about expense categories.

  — Be sure to include unusual expenses that may only occur once a year (such as moving costs, insurance or holiday gifts).

under-budget. Budgets are dynamic and they need to be reviewed regularly — and sometimes revised.

What do you do if your kid keeps running out of money every month? First, review the budget and actual spending to try to identify the problem area. If there is enough money to cover the basics, the fixed expenses, the problem may be discretionary spending on things like entertainment and eating out. Remember the three Cs: **CREATE**, **CONVERT** and **CONSERVE**. He may have to cut back on some of these expenses or make more money.

> *I got through university by taking full advantage of student discounts and always asking if there was a student rate for things like haircuts, gym memberships or theatre tickets. I also got into the habit of using coupons or two-for-one promotions when I went out for dinner with my friends. And whenever we felt like seeing a movie, we made sure to go to the "cheap Tuesday" shows!*

CREDIT CARDS REVISITED

Once your child has reached the age of majority in your province, she can get her own credit card. A credit card can be very helpful in case of emergency. (No, joining her friends for dinner or going shopping is not an "emergency"!) If your kid has been using *your* credit card for the last few years and is not the one paying the bills, they may be quite naïve about the responsible use of credit cards. If they get their own card, make sure the credit limit is low and try to find a card with no fees. Some cards even provide student discounts on purchases.

Credit is very easy to get and use. Many financial institutions offer credit cards specifically targeted to students, and they are marketed heavily on campuses. Paying by credit card is so convenient that it practically encourages spending. If you had to go to a bank and line up at the teller to take out cash every time you wanted to buy something, you would probably spend a lot less. These days, it's easy to withdraw cash from all the conveniently located ATMs, but it's even easier to just whip out a credit card and worry about it later.

Once again, the best way to teach your kids to use credit cards responsibly is to model this behaviour yourself. Let them know that you pay off your credit card balance each month. Explain to them that the credit card is used for convenience, but that it is a very expensive way to buy things you can't afford.

> *I was really happy about the new regulations requiring credit card companies to provide information on the time it would take to fully repay the balance if only the minimum payment is made every month. I read my kids the paragraph at the top of my most recent monthly statement for my credit card which charges 20% interest: 'The estimated time to pay your $1,526.57 balance in full if you pay only the Minimum Payment each month is: 12 years and 2 months.' That's a rude awakening—my kids were in a state of shock—I think the message really hit home!*

FAMILY DISCUSSION
Credit cards

Make sure they understand the basics of credit card use:

- Credit cards let you make purchases, up to a pre-determined credit limit, that are billed at a later date.
- Ideally, you pay off the balance on the due date every month. If not, you must make a minimum payment every month, and unpaid balances are subject to interest charges based on an annual percentage rate (or APR).
- The APR on some cards can be as high as 20%. Most cards also charge an annual fee and there are fees and penalties for late or missed payments.

Discuss the benefits of credit cards:

- They are convenient and practical.
- They allow you to create a credit history and earn a credit rating.
- They let you earn rewards, such as frequent flyer miles or cash-back payments.
- They are the only method of paying for online purchases.

Discuss the risks and disadvantages of credit cards:

- They can damage your credit rating if you miss payments or your payments are late.
- They are more expensive than personal lines of credit because the interest rate charged is much higher.
- If not used responsibly, credit cards can lead to increased spending and "bad debt".

THINGS TO DO/NOT TO DO
Identify theft

- Never provide personal information to anyone unless you know and trust the person and understand why they need it.
- Never email your personal information.
- Keep documents such as birth certificates, passports or Social Insurance Number cards in a secure and safe place—not in your wallet.
- Only use secure websites.
- Update your anti-virus software regularly.
- Shred all documents that include your personal financial information, e.g., old bank statements and credit card statements.

THINGS TO DO/NOT TO DO
Credit and debit card fraud

- Get a credit/debit card with "chip" technology. The embedded microchip is encrypted and virtually impossible to replicate.
- Do not share your credit/debit card or PIN.
- Never leave your credit/debit card unattended (or in your car's glove compartment) and make sure you get it back after payment.
- Cover the keypad when entering your PIN.
- Check your statements every month (or more frequently online) for errors or unauthorized transactions. Notify your bank or other financial institution immediately if something is amiss.
- Destroy cards you no longer need or use.

If you feel your child is ready for the responsibility of a credit card, encourage him to take the time to choose the right credit card. The Financial Consumer Agency of Canada has excellent resources about credit cards and other financial topics available at **www.fcac-acfc.gc.ca/eng/consumers/creditcard/index-eng.asp**.

FRAUD, SCAMS AND IDENTITY THEFT

Fraud can take many forms, including scams involving fake emails or websites, identity theft, credit card fraud and debit card fraud. Anyone can be a victim of fraud, and it is often costly—in terms of financial losses and the time it takes to clear your record. Teach your young adult how to protect herself and her financial information with the following tips.

Preventing identity theft

Identity theft occurs when your personal information or identity is stolen for the purpose of accessing your financial accounts to steal your assets or incur debt in your name. Take precautions to protect your personal information at home, in public, on the phone and online.

Preventing credit or debit card fraud

Credit and debit card fraud occurs when your credit/debit card information or your PIN is stolen and used to make unauthorized purchases or transactions.

A note about social media

The popularity of social media sites makes it very easy for fraudsters to obtain personal information that can be used to decode passwords. Also, announcing your upcoming vacation or attendance at an event on a specific evening is like drawing a map to an empty apartment or house. You may come home to find your valuables missing, including the valuable personal information someone needs to steal your identity.

SHARE

VOLUNTEERING YOUR TIME

Most students don't have much money for themselves, let alone enough to give away to others. But sharing isn't always about money—sometimes it's about volunteering your time and talents to help others. The idea of community service is not new—most students are now required to do some volunteering in order to graduate from high school. Although it's not usually mandatory in post-secondary studies, many students, despite the time pressures from their studies, choose to volunteer for two reasons—because volunteering aligns with their values and because of the many benefits they receive. Depending on the type of volunteer work they do, students can expand their network, learn new skills, gain work-related experience, have an adventure and feel good about giving back.

When looking for volunteer work, one of the most important considerations is passion. If your child doesn't already know what he or she is passionate about, ask them to complete or review their Values Validator (at the end of Chapter 1). This exercise will help them clarify what's really important to them, which will lead them to causes or organizations that they really care about. When you are not being paid for your time and efforts, passion is essential in order to remain committed. Before your child commits to a specific organization, it's a good idea for them to make sure they know exactly what the organization is expecting from them in terms of the nature and quantity of work involved. Depending on how formal the organization is, they may even want to get it in writing, so there are no misunderstandings later on.

PHILANTHROPY IS A FAMILY AFFAIR

In families where philanthropy is a key family value, the importance of sharing is taught at an early age and carried through to young adulthood.

When my kids were young, they each had a charity piggy bank and part of their allowance always went in there. When they became older, I set up a donor-advised fund to provide more structure to their giving. (A donor-advised fund is a charitable-giving vehicle administered by a third party to manage charitable donations on behalf of a family.) Each of my kids, aged 19 and 21, worked with a donor advisor and also attended a seminar to help them identify their philanthropic leanings. My daughter used her portion to sponsor raincoats for schoolchildren living in the rain-soaked mountains of Ecuador. My son, who played saxophone for his school band, supported a music program at a local school for at-risk children.

INVEST

LONG-TERM INVESTING: START EARLY AND INVEST REGULARLY

Some people at this age, whether they are in university or working full time, have more money than they need to cover their ongoing current expenses. The temptation is to see any extra funds as spending money, but it's a good idea to earmark some of it for investment. Emerging adults have decades ahead of them to invest, which gives them a huge advantage: time. Encourage your kid to start early and invest regularly, even if the amounts are small.

Emma Taylor began saving $5 each week when she was 15. Assuming Emma earned a 5% compound annual return, at 65 she would have $57,152. If she waited 10 years and didn't start until age 25, she would have $32,978.34 at age 65. And if she waited even longer, until she was 35 and saved for 30 years, she would have only $18,137.81.

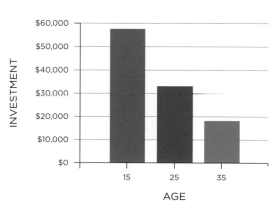

See also Advantages of Early Investing Calculator: **www.fiscalagents.com/ toolbox/cal/invest/aoei.shtml**

When investing for a long-term goal, a much longer time horizon means you can choose investments with growth potential. Take advantage of time and let compounding work *for* you, as we saw in Chapter 4. Depending on your tolerance for risk, you may have many different investment options.

STOCKS, BONDS AND OTHER INVESTMENTS

There are three traditional categories or classes of investments: cash, bonds and stocks. There are other types of investments, such as real estate, precious metals like gold and silver, and investments in private businesses. But when teaching your young adult, focus on the three traditional ones — the others are generally for more sophisticated investors with substantial investable assets. In investing, there is a direct relationship between risk and return. Lower-risk investments, like cash or bonds, have lower returns. Higher-risk investments, like stocks, have the potential to earn higher returns.

Your child may have learned some of these concepts in a high school business class, but it doesn't hurt to review the basics if she shows interest.

FAMILY DISCUSSION
Investments

Bonds:

- Explain that bonds are simply IOUs—they are debts issued by companies or governments.

- They usually pay a fixed or floating rate of interest to the investor for a specific period of time, called the "term".

- The interest rate is expressed as a percentage of the investment.

- Bonds issued by governments in the developed world are generally thought to be safe investments and, if the government has a good track record, the interest rate you earn will be relatively low compared to bonds issued by entities that are considered riskier.

- Remember: low risk = low reward.

Stocks:

- Explain that stocks represent an ownership stake in a company.

- The owners of a company's stock are called shareholders.

- Some stocks are traded on public stock exchanges, and their prices are determined by buyers and sellers.

- Stock prices can be quite unpredictable in the short-run: they can go up or down, and there are no guarantees regarding the safety of your investment or the return of your original capital. You could double your money, lose your entire investment, or come out anywhere in between. For this reason, stocks are said to be risky.

- You wouldn't buy stocks if you're investing for a short-term goal: you won't have enough time to recover if the stock price falls drastically right before you need the money.

Everyone has to assess their own comfort with risk. Some investors are very comfortable owning a high-risk portfolio while others are very uncomfortable with the gyrations of the market and the possibility of losing their principal. But if you are willing to take some risk by owning stocks, the potential returns are also higher than they are with less risky investments like GICs or bonds. Publicly traded stocks are also very liquid, meaning you can sell them at the prevailing market price quite quickly and easily.

When you own stocks you can earn investment income in two ways: dividends and capital gains (or losses). Dividends represent a proportionate share of the profits of a company and are paid by some companies to their shareholders; the decision about whether to pay a dividend on common shares (and how much to pay) is made by a company's board of directors. A capital gain is the difference between what you pay for an investment and what you sell it for, less any transaction costs. If the difference is positive, you have a gain; if it's negative, you have a capital loss.

THE BENEFITS OF DIVERSIFICATION

I'm sure at one time or another, for various reasons, you've advised your kids "not to put all your eggs in one basket". That lesson also applies to investing. Diversification is an investment strategy that aims to maximize returns while minimizing risk by choosing a mix of investments that will perform independently of one another so that some investments in your portfolio will have gains at times when others will have losses. It is the opposite of a much riskier strategy that chooses to concentrate on one asset class or even one security.

ASSET ALLOCATION AND SECURITY SELECTION

Once your young adult knows what he wants to achieve and when, he can decide how to achieve it with the proper asset allocation and securities. Asset allocation is the process of determining how the money in your investment portfolio should be divided among the different categories of investments: stocks, bonds, cash, real estate and others. Getting the asset allocation right for the investor's circumstances

THINGS TO DO
Investment plan

Before moving on to the next steps of asset allocation and security selection, ask your child to answer the following three questions. Writing the answers down will help them create an investment plan:

- What are your investment objectives?

- What is your time horizon?

- What is your risk tolerance?

is crucial because, according to the oft-quoted Brinson, Hood, and Beebower study, it accounts for over 90% of the variability of the returns on a typical investor's portfolio. Contrary to popular belief, it is a much more important step than security selection. Security selection accounts for only 4.6% of the variability. But people tend to focus on picking stocks and other securities because it is "sexier" and may give them something to brag about!

A tale of three investors

The Taylors are moderate investors who are most comfortable with a balanced portfolio: 50% stocks, 40% bonds and 10% cash.

Their friends, the Bennetts, have a greater appetite for risk and prefer to hold a more aggressive portfolio: 70% stocks, 20% bonds and 10% cash.

Their friend Carol is widowed and is ultra-conservative. She is very risk averse and although she will have a small pension, she is only comfortable owning GICs.

Let's assume that they each invest $100,000 and plan to reinvest any investment income they earn. How can we expect their portfolios to perform after 5 years, 10 years and 20 years?

Generally, ultra-conservative portfolios will grow very slowly and, although there is no risk that you will lose your principal, there is a risk that the returns will not outpace inflation and that therefore you may outlive your money. This is in fact what happened to Carol. Although she was outperforming the other two portfolios after 5 years and staying even after 10, she fell far behind after 20 years. As the Taylors and the Bennetts experienced, a more aggressive asset mix means more growth potential but also more likelihood of experiencing losses. In this example, the stock market was volatile in the first 10 years, and the more aggressive portfolios didn't really start to perform well until the second decade.

Investor	Portfolio	Initial Investment	After 5 years	After 10 years	After 20 years	Average annual return:
Carol	Ultra conservative	$100,000	$161,049	$236,206	$356,484	6.7%
Taylor	Balanced	$100,000	$154,330	$236,103	$424,785	7.5%
Bennett	Aggressive	$100,000	$129,503	$236,736	$560,441	9.0%

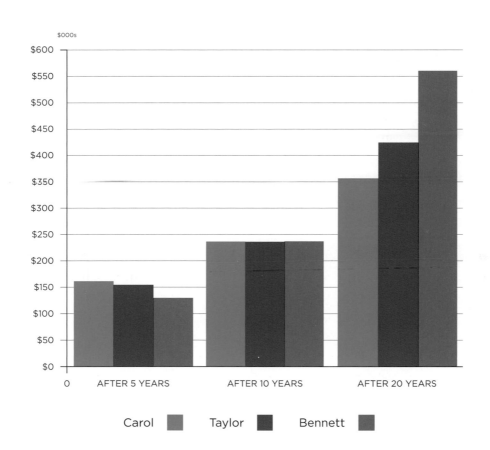

KEY POINTS

- Young adults become increasingly independent from you, but you can still have a lot of influence on them—they're often more willing to discuss important matters with you than they were just a few years earlier.

- Help them see that their new-found independence involves both privileges and responsibilities, i.e., they can work at more interesting jobs that pay them more, and as students they are entitled to certain tax breaks, but they have to file an income tax return to make sure they're taking full advantage of everything they're entitled to.

- Volunteering is a great way for young people to put their values into action, and it pays dividends in terms of real-world experience and personal satisfaction.

- It's a good idea to make sure they have good, basic investment knowledge. Some may already be in a position to start a portfolio; others will benefit from knowing what their options are when they do start to invest.

Resources

POST-SECONDARY STUDENT BUDGET[1]

Budget Calculator

This form will take about five minutes to complete. Please fill in as many of the fields below as possible with your household after-tax values to ensure an accurate estimate of the total budget you'll need.

INCOME		
Record or estimate your annual after-tax income from the following sources.		
Salary / Wages	$	Monthly/Annually
Self-employment / Business income	$	Monthly/Annually
Scholarships / Bursaries	$	Monthly/Annually
Parental contributions	$	Monthly/Annually
Other	$	Monthly/Annually
Total Income	$	

...continued

1   www.rbcroyalbank.com/student/medical/budgetcalculator/

Resources

POST-SECONDARY STUDENT BUDGET (continued)

EXPENSES

Estimate your expenses for the items listed, either as monthly or yearly values. If you are not sure how much to allocate for a given item, it may be helpful to record all your expenses for an entire month before returning to complete this form.

FOOD/HOUSING:

Food	$	Monthly/Annually
Mortgage or rent	$	Monthly/Annually
Other Housing costs	$	Monthly/Annually
Utilities	$	Monthly/Annually
Moving Costs	$	Monthly/Annually
Other	$	Monthly/Annually
Total Food and Housing	$	

TRANSPORTATION

Car Payments	$	Monthly/Annually
Insurance / License / Registration	$	Monthly/Annually
Service / Repairs / Gasoline	$	Monthly/Annually
Public Transportation / Parking	$	Monthly/Annually
Other	$	Monthly/Annually
Total Transportation	$	

...continued

Resources

POST-SECONDARY STUDENT BUDGET (continued)

EDUCATION		
Tuition	$	Monthly/Annually
Books / Subscriptions / Instruments	$	Monthly/Annually
Exam fees	$	Monthly/Annually
Professional fees	$	Monthly/Annually
Malpractice insurance	$	Monthly/Annually
Conferences	$	Monthly/Annually
Other	$	Monthly/Annually
Total Education	$	
INVESTMENTS AND SAVINGS		
RRSP contributions	$	Monthly/Annually
Conferences	$	Monthly/Annually
Other	$	Monthly/Annually
Total investments and savings	$	

...continued

Resources

POST-SECONDARY STUDENT BUDGET (continued)

LIFESTYLE/LOANS		
Credit payments	$	Monthly/Annually
Government student loan payments	$	Monthly/Annually
Insurance	$	Monthly/Annually
Uninsured health services	$	Monthly/Annually
Clothing / Dry Cleaning / Grooming	$	Monthly/Annually
Leisure Activities	$	Monthly/Annually
Child care	$	Monthly/Annually
Travel	$	Monthly/Annually
Other	$	Monthly/Annually
Total Lifestyle/Loans	$	
Total Expenses	$	

Resources

RESOURCES

CICA Financial Literacy Website:

> www.financialdecisionsmatter.com

Canadian Bankers' Association:

> www.yourmoney.cba.ca/

ABC Life Literacy Canada:

> www.abclifeliteracy.ca/tips-and-activities

Government websites:

> www.mint.ca
>
> www.currencymuseum.ca
>
> www.bankofcanada.ca/en/banknotes/index.html
>
> www.ic.gc.ca/eic/site/bsf-osb.nsf/eng/h_br01548.html
>
> www.fcac-acfc.gc.ca/

Additional info on RESPs:

> www.canlearn.ca/eng/saving/cesg/index.shtml
>
> www.cra-arc.gc.ca/tx/ndvdls/tpcs/resp-reee/menu-eng.html

Investor Education Fund:

> www.getsmarteraboutmoney.ca

Online tools for kids:

> www.theglobeandmail.com/globe-investor/personal-finance/
> smart-cookies/raise-money-smart-kids-with-these-online-tools/
> article1669238/

Send us ideas and anecdotes:

> moneysmartkids@cica.ca

ABOUT THE AUTHOR

Robin Taub is an experienced Chartered Accountant and a leader in the field of financial literacy.

She graduated with a Bachelor of Commerce degree from the Rotman School of Management at the University of Toronto and earned her Chartered Accountant designation in 1989. She went on to complete the Canadian Institute of Chartered Accountants' (CICA) In-Depth Tax Course in 1991. Robin values lifelong learning and in 2010 she participated in the Canadian Board Diversity Council's Director Education Program.

Robin has held professional positions at two of Canada's largest accounting firms, and spent five years in the complex world of Derivatives Marketing at Citibank Canada. Currently, she works with various organizations to create unbiased financial information, programs and resources to help Canadians make more informed and appropriate financial and investing decisions.

Robin is also passionate about improving opportunities for women CAs to advance into positions of leadership and is Chair of the Canadian Institute of Chartered Accountant's Women's Leadership Council.

Robin is the mother of two teenage children. She lives in Toronto and enjoys an active family life including biking, hiking, snowboarding, music, travel and reading.

You can learn more about Robin by visiting **www.robintaub.com**.

ACKNOWLEDGEMENTS

I would like to thank the following people at CICA who have helped me to make this book a reality:
- Cairine Wilson, Vice-President, Member Services, for giving me the opportunity to write this book, for her confidence in my abilities and her support throughout the process.
- Karen Duggan, Principal, Guidance & Support, for recommending me for this project.
- Maggie Tyson, CICA's Manager, Editorial Development, for her enthusiasm for the project and her many suggestions that made the book even better.
- Michael Dave Dizon, Art Director, for his innovative design.

I would also like to thank my editor, Tom Churchill, for his encouragement and positive feedback every step of the way.

Finally, I would like to thank my family and friends for their interest and support, my husband, Jonathan, for his admiration and encouragement in taking on this challenge, and my two children, Justin and Natalie, for providing a lot of the material for this book!

CICA and I would like to thank the Royal Bank of Canada for contributing some of the practical resources throughout this work.

— Robin Taub